The Blaming and Shaming
of Defenseless Victims
in America's Rape Culture

The Blaming and Shaming of Defenseless Victims in America's Rape Culture

Lisa R. Smith

LEXINGTON BOOKS
Lanham • Boulder • New York • London

Published by Rowman & Littlefield
An imprint of The Rowman & Littlefield Publishing Group, Inc.
4501 Forbes Boulevard, Suite 200, Lanham, Maryland 20706
www.rowman.com

86-90 Paul Street, London EC2A 4NE

British Library Cataloguing in Publication Information Available

Library of Congress Cataloging-in-Publication Data
978-1-7936-2709-4
978-1-7936-2711-7
978-1-7936-2710-0

Thanks to my brother, sisters, cousins, and my legions of students who inspired me to write this book

Your experiences and traumas were not ignored

~

Contents

~

Preface

My Introduction to Rape Culture

As a naive college student growing up on Long Island, NY, I learned about rape culture early. College life allowed me to live in co-ed dorms. There were comedy shows, movie nights, and a host of parties that we could attend in order to make connections with the mates of our choosing easier. In one of my sociology classes, it was said, "that the hidden curriculum of college life was to help us find a mate." When we weren't studying or partying our life away, we were at clubs doing devilish things, like drinking, smoking (cigarettes and weed), and looking for new lovers. Some of us would be looking for long-term lovers, and yet some of us would be looking for that short-term hookup that would often end in jilted feelings. It was clear that college life meant sexual freedom, but it also had hidden dangers. It was here that I learned that college life also meant the potential for rape of young unassuming victims.

On one such occasion, one of my best friends at the time, asked me to come over to her house for a visit. Her mother and siblings weren't home, her boyfriend and his friends were hanging out at her house, and we were going to watch the basketball game—the Knicks versus "who knows."

Me and good friend from school went over to her house to watch the game and hang out. It was clear that there were three guys and three girls and these boys were interested in more than watching the game. Luckily (I call myself lucky), I had a boyfriend at the time, so that X'ed me out of the equation for sex with these guys. When my friend and the guy she was with became intimate, I left the room and went to sleep on the couch.

My best friend was in another room with her boyfriend so I fell asleep. I was later awakened, in the middle of the night, by my college friend who was like "Lisa, get up, we have to go now." Not knowing what happened and seeing that there was a sense of urgency I quickly got up, we left the house, we got in the car, and on the way back to school she began to tell me what happened.

She admitted that although she was kissing, touching, she was clear that she did not want to have sex with him. When he became aggressive, starting to hold her down, managing to pull off her clothes, and then penetrate her, she knew she wasn't strong enough to stop the rape. As soon as it was over, and he released his grip, she left the room and came looking for me.

Listening to her story, I felt awful. One reason is because this was my best friend's house. Another reason is because I brought her to this environment, but last was because I fell asleep and left her in the room alone with him, thus making her vulnerable. When we got back to school, she and I did not discuss the sexual assault, but my best friend did not believe the rape truly happened. That was my shameful introduction into the world of rape culture, and I did and said nothing. My actions continue to haunt me to this day.

I write this book because although America's sexual assault and rape culture is well-known, there is a bastion of people that don't know what academics know about the role that blaming the victim plays in the maintenance of rape culture. Some wish to silence a victim's narrative as a lie or too graphic because it may make them uncomfortable or trigger them. But the rape myth, scripts, and the intersectionality of race, gender, class in conjunction with patriarchal institutions that systematically help perpetuate this epidemic and leave communities struggling to determine the best practices that should be implemented when sex crimes occur. I write this book for the legions of youth, students in psychology, sociology, and criminal justice courses, families, friends, and acquaintances that are not aware of the implicit biases that they hold associated with shame and doubt when dealing with sexual violence and victimization of vulnerable populations. I expect that this book will educate the masses and challenge them to consider that a victim of sexual assault or rape is telling the truth, and the first goal is to listen, and then take action to help reduce the number of undetected rapists roaming our streets.

Introduction

For decades, the United States has had a poor history with few prosecutions and convictions for sexual violent crimes. This book will serve as an indictment of the factors that contributed to the current rape epidemic as a result of collective memory of rape myths, schema, and scripts, loosely defined rape laws, failure of law enforcement's submission of sexual assault kits for testing (Patterson, 2011; Kaiser, O'Neal, & Spohn, 2017; Campbell & Fehler-Cabral, 2018), limits of victim reporting and credibility (Hlavka, 2014), and the social institutions that adopted denial, inaction, and information suppression with non-disclosure agreements (Ence, 2019). Today, three out of four sexual assaults will not be reported because victims fear reprisal, law enforcement agents' judgment and inaction, or that the allegations would cause harm to the offender (Rape, Abuse & Incest National Network, 2019). Every sixty-eight seconds, an American is sexually assaulted, yet five out of one thousand rapists will be jailed for their crimes. This indicates that there are undetected rapists living with impunity in our communities (Lisak & Miller, 2002; Lisak, 2006; Valentine, et al., 2016; Campbell & Fehler-Cabral, 2018). Sexual violence impacts vulnerable segments of society that include children, teens, LGBTQ youth, women, military personnel, people with disabilities, and prisoners with limited agency who are subjected to the intersections of oppression. This book is structured around two main questions: Does the intersectionality of status, race, gender, and age play a significant role in the blame the victim syndrome that prevents the elimination and eradication of this epidemic, and how is victim blaming used to normalize sexual violent stereotypes that blame and shame defenseless victims?

> Sexual violence can never be completely eradicated until we have successfully affected a whole range of radical social transformations in our country . . . To recognize the larger sociopolitical context of the contemporary epidemic of sexist violence does not, however, mean that we ignore the specific and concrete necessity for the ongoing campaign against rape. This battle must be waged quite concretely on all its myriad of fronts. As we further shape the theoretical foundation of the anti-rape movement and as we implement practical tasks, let us constantly remind ourselves that even as individual victories are claimed, the complete elimination of sexist violence will ultimately depend on our ability to forge a new and revolutionary global order, in which every form of oppression and violence against humankind is obliterated. (Davis, 1989, p. 49–51)

This quote by Angela Davis describes the social problem of rape as a "contemporary epidemic," [in which its] complete eradication requires social change in the sociopolitical arenas on the micro (family) and macro levels (institutions, organizations and networks) of society. It also points to the need for "radical social transformations" that have emerged from the grassroots efforts of the #MeToo movement that illuminated the normalization of sexual violence that created a pervasive rape culture in cities (urban, suburban, and rural) throughout America (Hlavka, 2014). When a society normalizes the social problem of intimate traumas such as rape and sexual assault abuses, it means that collectively, members (families, institutions, organizations) have informally agreed to adopt feelings, beliefs, and behaviors that become a standard or common practice that people learn to gradually accept over time as a collective memory (Mary & Senn, 1995). A social problem is defined as a "condition" in which a large number of people identify the problem as a "deviation" from beloved social norms or treasured mores (Fuller & Myers, 1941) that is "intrinsically harmful or malignant . . . in contrast to a normal or socially healthful society"(Blumer, 1971). It consists of both an "objective condition and subjective definition" that has a natural history of evolution (Fuller & Myers, 1941; Blumer, 1971; Mary, Senn, 1995).

With the objective condition, it must be recognized by experts (i.e., trained observers, researchers, community leaders, legislators) that use impartial protocols that can verify the existence of the problem with empirical observations and methods (Fuller & Myers, 1941). Sociocultural values are equally important because they serve as the subjective definition where members of society label rape culture and see the issue as a fundamental threat to existing normative dimensions of humanity. Each social problem has a "natural history" (awareness, policy determination, and reform) in which the issue develops slowly over time as a result of intersectionality of inequalities within society (i.e., race, gender, age) that cause the social problem to be ignored (Mary & Senn, 1995).

Fuller & Myers (1941) theorized that these sociocultural values can serve dual roles: (a) an "important causal role; and (b) obstruct solutions." America's rape culture is preserved when members of society and institutions cling to the prejudices of rape myths, societal beliefs of gender sexual scripts, victim credibility, offender blameworthiness and share these messages with others. Addressing the epidemic forces societal members to dismantle their preconceptions about sexual violence, embrace the notions that rape culture exists, then adopt and enact viable solutions (i.e., programs and policies) to eradicate its existence. Feminist theories have helped fuel the current #MeToo culture.

The Intersection of Feminism and #MeToo

Since the late 1970s, feminist theories have pressed for gender equality and the dismantling of misogynistic, patriarchal systems (Gillespie, Mirabella, & Eikenberry, 2019). Radical feminism exposed the gender inequities that are associated with the intersection of the power and status of men. Scholars believe that the subjugation of women, sexual violence and rape are the remnants of the male dominated culture (Phipps, 2018). With liberal feminism, social institutions where gender discrimination was most prevalent and social change was necessary for women to receive equitable pay and parity would provide new guidance for feminism in the postmodern era (Atkinson, 2014). The demand for sociopolitical ideologies that address feminine cultural and economic agency could be established to create social justice movements that promoted new ideas of self-efficacy and social change. The #MeToo movement became the basis for the radical feminist social change that would be needed to hold powerful men and the institutions they headed accountable for sexual harassment and sexual violence that would later change policies, laws, and build advocacy allies that could combat the rape myths, schema, and scripts of past eras. But some believe that several populations were left out of the #MeToo movement (Reingold, 2017). This includes black men, transgender, intersex, Asians (the fetishizing of females), Native Americans, people with disabilities, sex workers and other marginalized groups that are victims of sexually violent attacks. As #MeToo continues to evolve, the spotlight can be shined on countless numbers of victims from all sociocultural groups that have survived rape or sexual assault, demand accountability, and pursue prosecution that addresses the social cost and risk to others by reducing the number of undetected rapists.

The goal of this book is to:

1. Discuss the evolution of America's rape culture
2. Establish the link between prejudices of rape myths from societal members (victims, offenders, police, prosecutors, etc.) and the focal concerns perspective that includes (a) offender blameworthiness, (b) desire to protect the community from threat, and (c) imposition of constraints and consequences that result in few convictions and the blaming and shaming of victims
3. Introduce a new theory (denial, inaction, information suppression [DIIS]) that constructs the foundation of victim blame to establish the societal and institutional legitimization of sexual violence against defenseless and vulnerable victims

Focal Concerns Theory

The focal concerns theory is widely used in the criminal justice field as part of judges' decision-making process during the conviction and sentencing of offenders which provides three areas of concern (Steffensmeier, Ulmer, & Kramer, 1998). Focal concerns explain how various members the of community (victims, police, prosecutors, judges) have used three major focal concerns associated with sex assault and rape that include: (a) offender blameworthiness, (b) desire to protect the community from threat, and (c) imposition of constraints and consequences that result in convictions. This theoretical perspective linked with current rape myth acceptance results in the blaming and shaming of victims and generates questions regarding their credibility thus preventing their cooperation in prosecutions and convictions (Steffensmeier, Ulmer, & Kramer, 1998; Patterson, 2011; Campbell & Fehler-Cabral, 2018). Focal concerns theory can be applied to America's rape culture. Victims that were intoxicated or used illegal substances may blame themselves or may not believe that the offender would be prosecuted thus influencing the offender's blameworthiness (Campbell & Fehler-Cabral, 2018). This can reduce the victims' decisions to cooperate with law enforcement (Patterson, 2011; Kaiser, O'Neal & Spohn, 2017). Though, victims are concerned with keeping others safe from the offender's predation, they are also concerned that substance usage and losing consciousness during the attack may impact their ability to prosecute the offender if they forget specific details. Additional victim's concerns may be associated with rape myths that include their dress code, location of the assault, misread messages of consent, or past relationship with the offender (Campbell & Raja, 1999; Campbell & Ferhler-Cabral, 2018). Their final concern is the potential of prosecution. Will their version of the story be believed and will the offender's status (socioeconomic status, race, gender, age) play a role in prosecution? Will the circumstances that led to the sexual assault influence the police decision to submit the sexual assault kit, prosecutors' willingness to prosecute and a possible conviction?

Last, how will these circumstances affect a judges' ruling and sentencing. Police have similar focal concerns and engage in similar decision-making processes. Their views are important because members of law enforcement (i.e., detectives) are the gatekeepers that make the decisions to investigate rapes and later submit their findings to prosecutors for potential conviction. The first concern is affected by offender blameworthiness, and they may compare the rape of strangers to nonstranger sexual assaults. Legal factors such as severity or lethality of assault, gang rape, physical injury, and strength of evidence play a significant role in the decision-making process for law enforcement. Extralegal factors are also considered (a) victim's behavior prior to the assault, (b) victim demographics, (c) suspect demographics, (d) victims' "credibility," (e) drug usage, (f) mental health disclosure, and other factors.

Denial, Inaction, Information Suppression (DIIS Theory)

Within the African American colloquy, to be consistently disrespected by others is to be "dissed," insulted, and ultimately dismissed (Cambridge Dictionary, 2021). Survivors of sexual violence have experienced this phenomenon of the repeated "diss" and ultimate disrespect. This societal disrespect is observed at the micro and macro levels of society and is the foundation for denial, inaction, information suppression or DIIS Theory. When an offender lies about raping his childhood friend, or an emergency room nurse refuses to take DNA samples for a rape kit, the survivor is dissed. When friends and family members deny a sexually violent act and ignore the truth, the survivor is dissed and dismissed. Corporations or organizations that fail to investigate sexual assault or university investigations require the use of non-disclosure agreements; survivors are dissed. One of the negative effects for sexual assault and rape victims is lack of support and denial from a network of people and institutions that includes parents, family, friends, social service providers, law enforcement, churches, and so on.

Denial is defined as a psychological defense mechanism that a person uses to screen out distressing realities and the painful feelings they cause (Adams, 1994). It is detrimental to the rape survivor because it allows the denier to blame, shame, "re-rape and re-victimize" victims because support and validation of the sexual violent crime is withheld (Campbell & Raja, 1999). Denial provides insight that explains the psyche of the denier (Raphael, 2013). In the case of a mother that denies the sexual assault of a child, Adams (1994) explains that it "protects her from the pain of knowing about the abuse, from ensuing feelings of anger and betrayal towards [the abuser], and from her feeling of guilt for not having protected her child." However, when a social service practitioner engages in denial, it leads to "victim blaming, insensitivity, and the denial of a victim's account or of much needed services (counseling, pregnancy and STI testing, and legal prosecution (Campbell, & Raja, 1999). Denial is connected to inaction when examining institutional responses to sexual violent claims (Phipps, 2018).

Like denial, inaction is part of re-victimization when the institution fails to investigate the crime, punish the offender, neglects to provide consequences, or fails to protect the victim from further abuses (Campbell & Fehler-Cabral, 2018). Examples of inaction can be applied to institutions like:

a. The Roman Catholic Church (Dunne, 2011) when felonious priests and nuns remained at the parish or were moved to another parish which resulted in continued sexual abuse
b. Allegations of a growing number of suspected Boy Scouts leaders' pedophilic offenses were documented and stored in the "Perversion Files" which contained list of approximately 7,800 pedophiles but many remained in their role as scout leaders (Shattuck, Finkelhor, Turner, & Hamby, 2016)
c. The Chicago Public School system needed intervention from the Department of Education in order to monitor the mishandling of hundreds of sexual assaults which occurred between 2012-2019 (Hobbs, 2019; Masterson, 2020)

Information suppression accompanies denial and inaction and can be defined as systematic methods used to quiet victims of sexual violence complaints. This can be seen at the macro levels of society when law enforcement detectives fail to submit DNA evidence (hair, fibers, blood, semen, etc.) collected from sexual assault kits (SAKs). Currently, a nationwide backlog exists in which 200,000+ SAKs were not submitted for forensic lab testing. Failure to obtain DNA evidence after a sexual assault occurs is connected to information suppression and the second focal concern of keeping the public safe. The forensic labs can enter the evidence collected into the FBI's Combined DNA Index System (CODIS) for possible offender matches or match the DNA to other crimes (Campbell, Patterson, Bybee & Sworkin, 2009). And in the cases where the offenders are strangers, the undetected rapists are free to commit new offenses (Campbell, Patterson, Bybee & Sworkin, 2009; Campbell & Fehler-Cabral, 2018; Valentine, et al., 2016). Prosecutors also play an important role in the suppression of information because they determine the severity of the charges (if any), decide to indict an offender, and prepare the prosecutorial arguments (Campbell & Fehler-Cabral, 2018). But if they believe a victim's credibility will hinder a conviction, the decision to file criminal charges against an alleged rapist ends. More importantly, they have failed in their role and focal concern to keep the public safe while increasing the social cost to the community. Offenders are free to commit new sex crimes against unsuspecting victims. Institutional information suppression can be seen on the corporate and organization levels with the use of non-disclosure agreements (NDAs) in the Harvey Weinstein, Bill Cosby, and Larry Nassar cases.

NDAs (also known as non-disparagement agreements) prohibit the victim from disclosing details about the settlement or facts which led to the settlement in sexual assault or rape cases (Ence, 2019). Employers and human resource departments maintain the secrecy of employee's workplace conduct with use of NDAs which are often accompanied by mandatory arbitration agreements. These can be found embedded in employee handbooks and are necessary to aid the employer against an employee's potential lawsuit. A provisional request, employers use of "arbitration prevents these cases from entering the public realm of knowledge, shrouding the process in secrecy." It leads to undisclosed employee settlements but requires the victim to remain silent. In some cases, offenders are asked to complete trainings, others are fired. But arbitration agreements allow an assailant to obtain a new position, a promotion, or another job with an uninformed employer. Victims may have lost their job or experience criticism and ridicule when reporting claims. But within the past five years, America's pervasive rape culture was exposed by the #MeToo movement and the public outcry for social justice reforms have increased sociopolitical demands for change. Social change includes the reduction of denial, inaction, and information suppression (DIIS) at the micro and macro level. The theory suggests that if a family, friend, nurse, law enforcement agency, counselor, Title IX board, human resource manager, or board of directors engages in behaviors associated with the three steps of DIIS, a potential cover-up of the sex crime is expected.

With the introduction of DIIS theory, chapter 1 will provide a brief history of America's rape culture with comparisons that include Christian biblical passages of rape with sociopolitical practices found during colonial times through present day which were influenced by the intersection of race, gender, status, and age. Theoretical perspectives of focal concerns and DIIS theory are synthesized and applied to the societal perceptions of the time while noting the changes that affected prosecutions and sentencing. Next, chapter 2 will examine the current legal definitions of sexual violence, with comparisons to previous definitions that may have influenced social opinions, awareness, legislation, policies, and reform. Forms of sexual violence and rape will be discussed with application of statutes and sentencing minimums that explain the differences of sexual offender vs. predator. Law enforcement agencies indifference to the submission of sexual assault kits and their social perceptions of victim credibility based on their assessment of false, simple, and real rape (Estrich, 1987) will be assessed.

Chapter 3 will continue to provide theoretical analysis to explore the sexual abuse of children, incest, and different categorizations of sex offenders. Because grooming methods of sex offenders and predators that target and coerce children to engage in sexual encounters are different from those employed with teens and adolescents, a breakdown of the strategies will be provided and applied to recent scandals of the Roman Catholic and the Boy Scout of America organization. Chapter 4 will shift focus to adolescents and young adults, discuss the sexual predation approaches of assailants, and focal concern implications. Cautions regarding the Title IX challenges facing educational institutions university, and college policies will be addressed with the application of the DIIS theory to K-12 school districts located in Ashland Oregon and Redland Unified, California.

In chapter 5, using the DIIS theory, the intrapsychic effects and trauma from the victims of sexual assault and rape will be assessed. Also, the societal factors associated with perpetrators perspectives will also be applied to DIIS theory in order to address the motivations that may be attributed to recurring assaults and selection of potential victims.

Chapter 6 will explore the influence of social media and the rise of the #MeToo movement helped direct the sociopolitical awareness that Fuller & Myers (1941) identified as the natural progression of a social problem (awareness, policy determination, reform) in order to promote the radical social transformation that Davis (1989) believed would be needed for social change. Using focal concerns and the DIIS theoretical perspectives, a synthesis of cases that received national attention will be discussed using the intersectionality of status, gender of victims that were blamed and shamed with NDAs. Lastly, we will provide a path forward that includes the need for reform with the use of mandatory empathic trainings and collaborations with victim services in law enforcement institutions in order to amend the decision making processes that affects the submission of SAKs for forensic lab testing and prosecutorial ideas regarding victim credibility. Suggestions for future legislation that affect various institutions focal concerns, networks, and policy will also be examined.

To summarize, this discussion will examine the focal concerns theory of victims, law enforcement, societal institutions (micro/macro level), during the sexual violent crime investigation and prosecution process. Additionally, we hope to establish a link with the DIIS theory when sociopolitical institutions, organizations, and networks engage in denial, inaction, and information suppression in order to blame and shame victims. Societal rape stereotypes are analyzed based on the intersection of status, gender, and age that could be attributed to the reduction of convictions. It is important that radical social transformations are employed in order to help communities identify their undetected rapists in order to begin the eradication and elimination of sexual violent crimes in America.

CHAPTER ONE

~

America's Collective Memory, Religious Past, and Sexist Beliefs Contribute to Its Current Rape Culture

In the next sixty-eight seconds, someone in America will be sexually assaulted or raped. (Rape, Abuse, & Incest National Network, 2021). This grotesque, yet alarming statistic will be repeated in various chapters of this book because of the pervasive issue of sexual violence and the use of victim blaming in America's current rape culture (Bhuptani & Messman, 2021). Victim blaming is associated with two factors, false lies promoted by rape myth acceptance (RMA) linked to beliefs that the victim deserved it (sexual violence acceptance) and the gender differences that favor the notion that the offender did not intend to rape (Bhuptani & Messman, 2021; Rollero & Tartaglia, 2019). These historical rape myths can best be defined within the theoretical framework of collective memory.

Maurice Halbwach explained that collective memory encompasses an interdisciplinary approach that links individual memories with memories of social groups and historical facts of the past (Friedmann, 1946). These memories consist of cultural mores, religious beliefs, and traditions (sociology), artifacts (i.e., photographs, books), symbols (texts) and religious rituals (anthropology), national, sociopolitical (political science), and financial (economics) experiences that can include trauma (psychology) which may be embedded in laws, policies (criminal justice), that influence societal rules (Gensburger, 2016). Researchers state that collective memories are widely shared historical records and cognitive machinations that are dependent upon social interactions that can originate as memories of past events (i.e., wartime, family events, sporting events, etc.). Communities of people share memories through conversations, eyewitness accounts, recall from childhood memories, schemas, and ideas from media which can be defined as a "shared reality" based on repeated accounts of events (Brown, Kouri, & Hirst, 2012).

Although a society does not possess a memory, the collection of individual memories from social group members shapes the historical past and collective memory of America's rape culture. This includes language associated with rape myths and scripts, symbols, and mores linked to religious beliefs. Additionally, sexists' ideologies that can be attributed to the gender differences found in evolutionary psychology and religious schemas shared within social groups have transmitted these memories from one generation to the next.

The goal of this chapter is to explore the history of America's rape culture that often blames the victims while exposing the link between sexism and Christian religiosity. It will show the incongruence of earlier religious doctrine and beliefs regarding victims of rape and written biblical texts. A brief history of rape culture that spans from colonial times to the present will show a shift in belief systems that embrace victim blame and shame associated with patriarchy and sexism. The focal concerns theory will be used to analyze the intersection of status, gender, and race attributed to (a) an offender's blameworthiness, (b) protecting the community and (c) the cost of conviction and establishing an association with many of our social institutions' contribution to rape culture acceptance.

Victim Blame, Shame, and Religion

The blaming and shaming of victims of sexual violence is part of rape myth acceptance and current rape culture ideologies that can be traced to religious beliefs that devalue women (Moon & Reger, 2014). In the United States, approximately 75 percent of the population identify as Christian (i.e., Protestants (49 percent), Catholics (23 percent), Mormons (2 percent) (Newport, 2017). Barnett, Sligar, & Wang (2018) found that individuals with Protestant and Catholic religious' affiliations had high rape myth acceptance and were more likely to support the rapist and not the victim. Protestant and Catholic men were more likely to support rape myth acceptance than women. These stereotypes and prejudices are the basis for the foundational support of the current rape culture and rape myth acceptance that has plagued our U.S. society and reinforced the power differences of sexism. The dominant patriarchal beliefs and the sociocultural attitudes regarding biological sex, the social construct of gender, and sexuality contribute to the lies associated with rape myths (Barnett, Sligar, & Want, 2018; Haggard, Kaelen, Saroglou, Klein, & Rowatt, 2019). Research supports the correlation between rape myth acceptance, religiosity, and sexism (Prina & Schatz-Stevens, 2020). For centuries, cultural and societal beliefs have normalized various forms of sexism: (a) benevolent, (b) hostile, and (c) ambivalent (Glick & Ficke, 1997; Haggard, Kaelen, Saroglou, Klein, & Rowatt, 2019) that encourage rape myths.

Sexism

Benevolent sexism is defined as "an ideology that tempers relational costs, while maintaining men's power, by characterizing women as delicate, pure and in need of men's protection and care" (Hammond, Milojev, Huang, & Sibley, 2018). These ideals are fragments of the evolutionary psychological theories that were attributed to hunter gatherer societies where women were protected by the men in their lives (i.e., father, brother, husband), and when women leave the protection of these men, they do it at their own peril and jeopardize their survival (Davis, 2021). By the basis of their reproductive roles, women were nurturers, gathered edible foods close to home that they cooked for their men, nurtured, and cared for the children. Men hunted prey for food and their gender role of protector of the family was well established. divisions of labor, associated with mating and reproduction that began thousands of years ago helped shape the gender disparities and power dynamics seen in today's institutions of society (Zhu & Chang, 2019). Challenges to these beliefs that encourage women to cast aside traditional female roles of purity are contributing to hostile sexism (Moon & Reger, 2014). Haggard et al. (2019) conducted four studies in the United States and Belgium that found positive correlations between religious priming and benevolent sexism. Religious primers supported by stereotypical attitudes associated with rape myths. Moon & Reger (2014) used content analysis with Christian ideals to identify the stereotypes associated with rape myth acceptance. Some myths include (a) women as property, (b) the dehumanization of women, (c) abstinence before marriage, (d) the "blurred lines of sex and rape" as a hunt, or a prize to be won, (e) if a girl kisses or make's out with a guy, she wants to have sex, and (f) when a guy rapes, it's because he had a strong desire for sex (McMahon & Farmer, 2011).

Hostile sexism devalues women with biased, misogynistic beliefs in which women use sexual seduction in order to control men with manipulation. These seductresses tempt and tease men, with the possibility of receiving sex in order to cede power and once received, they refuse his sexual overtures (details of this topic will be discussed in chapter 5). Men have used these scenarios to fuel their anger to engage in aggressive sexual interactions that result in rape (McMahon & Farmer, 2011).

Glick & Fiske (1996) defined ambivalent sexism as the combination of both benevolent (positive) and hostile (negative) sexism embedded in current cultural values (Glick & Fiske, 2011; Moon & Reger, 2014; Haggard, Kaelen, Saraglou, Klein & Rowatt, 2019). Ambivalent sexism includes patriarchal dynamics in which men have more power and status than women. The social roles associated with gender encourage significant power differentials between men and women that affect parity that can also be contributed to sexual reproduction (Glick & Fiske, 2011). Men are viewed as the providers and protectors of women and children and possessing these views supports benevolent sexism. Research shows that those that possess benevolent sexism are more likely to blame and shame victims of sexual violent crimes (Rollero & Tartaglia, 2019). These notions support the idea that women are weaker, males exert more dominance with women within intimate relationships and sexual interactions, and women that challenge a male's power while seeking control experience hostile sexism (Prina & Schatz-Stevens, 2020; Rollero & Tartaglia, 2019). The fact that both men and women can hold all forms of sexism (overt, covert, and subtle) is the focus of rape culture and its normalization. Overt sexism is blatant, unequal and harmful to women, while covert sexism includes similar beliefs that are hidden. Subtle sexism is normalized but more harmful than overt and covert sexisms because both men and women who believe in gender equality hold negative views toward powerful women and feminists while holding positive views toward men in leadership roles (Swim & Cohen, 1997). In a study of 951 students, men and women were asked about their rape myth beliefs that included: She asked for it; It wasn't really rape; He didn't mean to; and She lied (McMahon & Farmer, 2011). Men were more likely to hold prejudiced rape myths about women, but women rejected these beliefs. Herman (1988) warned that U.S. society is a rape culture because it fosters and encourages rape by instructing citizens that it is normal and natural for sexual relations to involve aggressive behavior on the part of males. Herman goes on to say that as long as these types of relationships are supported, rape will remain a common occurrence. Studies show that people that display these various forms of sexism have higher rates of rape myth acceptance (Glick & Fiske, 2011; Rollero & Tartaglia, 2019).

Rape Myth Acceptance & Rape Scripts

When sexual assault and rape happens, societal perceptions differ on a wide spectrum based on the setting, the victim, the assailant and the intersection of race, class, and gender (Hockett, Saucier and Badke 2016). As rape myths and scripts continue to flood the American psyche, the terms "real rape and simple rape" are part of the colloquy and contribute to rape myth acceptance (Estrich, 1988). In order to meet the criteria for a "genuine" or *real rape* claim, the perpetrator must be a stranger, have used some form of force or physical violence, and/or a weapon against the victim (Du Mont, Miller, and Myhr 2003). Otherwise, the victim risks the classification that the sexual assault is a "false claim."

Additionally, the victim must show signs of emotional trauma, visible scars, bruises, and/or injuries (i.e., broken bones). If the victim was a virgin before the rape, her claim is most likely acknowledged because she was sexually inexperienced, chaste, and less likely to coerce her attacker with seduction (Hockett, Saucier and Badke 2016). In a Centers for Disease Control and Prevention study, conducted from 2011–2017 approximately 3.3 million women (ages eighteen to forty-four) reported that their first sexual experience was rape (Santhanam 2019). Seven percent of the women surveyed were under ten when the assault occurred, 29 percent were between eleven and fourteen and 39 percent were between fifteen and seventeen. If a victim is not a virgin and has had several sexual experiences and partners, is a prostitute, a sex worker, or has worked in the porn industry, her sexual assault will not be classified as a real rape. Rape myths and scripts minimize the seriousness of sexually violent attacks and blame the victim scenarios arise in conjunction with sexist beliefs (Prina & Schatz-Stevens, 2020). When defining rape myths and scripts, it is important to note that the societal views and prejudices are nested within each other and for this reason the terms are often used synonymously. *Rape myths* are defined as societal perceptions, "prejudices and stereotypes about victims, and rapists." (Hockett, Saucier and Badke 2016) Myths in which *victims* are blamed, shamed, and stereotyped include (Rollero & Tartaglia, 2019; Our Resistance, 2020):

- Provocative clothing and dress code was a factor that lead to the rape.
- When a victim is promiscuous, they are encouraging sexual violence.
- Going to a bar or club or walking by dark alleyways may have precipitated the rape.
- The victim was drinking or using other drugs which resulted in a sexual assault.
- A victim must fight back or have bruises for the act to be considered a sexual assault.
- Victims must be show signs of trauma by crying hysterically and display intense emotions.
- The victim never said no, so the assailant did not receive a clear message to stop.

- Prostitute and porn stars can't be raped.
- Men aren't victims of rape.
- Few people with disabilities are victims of sexual assault.
- Victims made a false claim.
- Women of color are considered sexually promiscuous, labeled Jezebels and hypersexed.

Myths and stereotypes that support the *perpetrator*'s behaviors and actions while ignoring the crime can include (Our Resilience, 2020):

- Males are hypersexed and can't control their lustful need for sex.
- A spouse or intimate partner can't rape because sex is consensual, not forced.
- Only strangers can rape.
- The perpetrator had to use coercion, physical force, or a weapon to commit rape.
- Serial rapists are not common.

Rape scripts are societal stereotypes about the rape setting, act of rape, or sexual violence (Hockett, Saucier and Badke 2016). These include (Our Resilience, 2020):

- Sexual assaults occur in isolated areas.
- Sexually violent crimes happen outside or in public.
- Violence and bruises must be visible in order call it rape.
- A weapon must be used for the act to be considered rape.

While many of these stereotypes are prejudices, they are often associated with victim blaming judgments and shaming (Hockett, Saucier, and Badke 2016). The prevalence of sexual violence in society, the number of people most likely affected by it, and the groups that are most vulnerable (children and teenage girls) to its occurrence dispels the belief of the Just World Theory and that somehow the victims "deserved the consequences" when they were intimately and violently raped (Roberts 2016). Does a five-year-old who is raped by her father deserve the attack? This social problem has existed for centuries and with all the progressive advancements (technological, social change policies, awareness and prevention programs), societal protections have not reduced the problem. Victim blaming helps "distort the facts" using lies, rape myths, and scripts that allow offenders to go free and survivors left with the burden of proof to supply the evidence to support their claims (Raphael 2013).

Blaming the Victim

When sexual victimization occurs, why do we blame the victim? Victim blame is a natural response to the receipt of uncomfortable information (Felson & Palmore, 2018). It is a consequence of the perception of recklessness and assumes that the victim engaged in wrongdoing. However, when the victim is a women, a member of a minority group, and part of a lower class, the intersectionality of these factors intensifies victim blame and shame (Sjöberg & Sarwar, 2020). With acquaintance rapes, victim blame is more likely to be assigned than when the perpetrator is a stranger (Gravelin, Biernat, & Bucher, 2019). Most importantly, people may not believe that the sexual assault or rape occurred and may dismiss or deny the victim's account of the events when the offender is not a stranger. RAINN (2021) statistics show that 93 percent of survivors of sexually violent crimes are acquaintances. With the majority of sex offenders identified as males, power dynamics associated with sexism become problematic. When coupled with religiosity and rape myth acceptance, victims blame ae blamed more often than they are believed (Reingold, #MeToo: Who is Being Left Out?, 2017). According to Christians, sexual violence is equivalent to the sexual sin of sex before marriage and ultimately, a consequence (Moon & Reger, 2014). But this is not how the ancient doctrine of the Hammurabi Code and the Bible addressed rape in its text.

Code of Hammurabi

In ancient Babylonia in the Mesopotamian region, the Hammurabi Code is considered one of the earliest forms of government (circa 1754 BCE) (Wells, 2013). Containing a list of 282 laws, it was devised by King Hammurabi in order to maintain social order and provide punishment for significant violations. Incest and rape were punishable offenses that violated the mores of primitive society in which perpetrators received severe penalties. In cases of incest, a father that sleeps with his daughter is exiled from the city (Section 154). If a father engaged in a sexual relationship with his son's wife, he was strangled and the wife was drowned in the Euphrates River (Section 155). However, if a mother and son were engaged in an incestuous relationship, they were burned (Section 157). Rape of a married women resulted in the perpetrator's death sentence and the woman was free to marry another or return to her father's home. Women were considered property, and the well-established patriarchal system enforced the notion that rape was a property crime with harsh punishments in the Code of Hammurabi (Allen, 2018). These social taboos were also punishable in biblical times.

Rape and the Bible

In the three cases of sexual assault found in the bible, rape is acknowledged, vengeance sought, and the death of the offender, the ultimate resolution (McCoy, 2015). In the biblical passages, the community, when made aware of the rape, did not ignore or silence the victim, but sought justice with the deaths of the larger community. The actions of the members of the community used the focal concerns theory on the micro and macro level. First, the offender's blameworthiness, culpability, and severity of the crime was not questioned. The perpetrator's innocence was not measured by his status, the amount of property he owned, and his social standing within the village. Second, is the focal concern of keeping the community safe or more specifically, the women of the community safe. Each man protects the victims. While men may consult others, or others may question their actions, the evidence is irrefutable, there must be a consequence to match the severity of the crime of rape. The last focal concern of accountability for the consequences of their decision and the social costs of the punishment must be considered. In these cases, the death of the offender is the sentence, but the social cost of the decisions to kill the offender caused war. War meant that other men would be held accountable for the actions of the offender and would die. In the case of war, shame was linked with the offender and his deeds which could cause the death of others. The rape myths that often accompany the victims of rape were not allied with the victim. The men did not blame or shame these women and willingly asked for help from other men to go to war in order to preserve the victims' dignity. This analysis can be found in the passages provided:

In Genesis 34, Dinah and Shechemites (Bible Gateway):

> Now Dinah, the daughter Leah had borne to Jacob, went out to visit the women of the land. When Shechem son of Hamor the Hivite, the ruler of that area, saw her, he took her and raped her. His heart was drawn to Dinah daughter of Jacob; he loved the young woman and spoke tenderly to her. And Shechem said to his father Hamor, "Get me this girl as my wife."
>
> When two of Dinah's brothers Simeon and Levi heard of the rape of their sister, they killed Shechem, Hamor and all the men of the city that Hamor ruled. Their reply to their father who was afraid that the actions of his sons would start a war was simple:
> "Should he have treated our sister like a prostitute?"

In Judges 19-21, a Levite from Ephraim traveling with his wife, concubine and servants back home sought shelter in the town of Gibeah of Benjamin.

When he was repeatedly turned down for shelter by the townsmen, he decided to sleep in the public square. An honest older man returning from his field work offered the Levite his home to stay for the night. However, the Levite recounts the events that led to the rape and murder of his concubine:

> It was at Gibeah of Benjamin, which my concubine and I had entered for the night. The lords of Gibeah rose up against me and surrounded me in the house at night. I was the one they intended to kill, but they abused my concubine and she died.
> The rape and murder of the Levite's concubine led to a civil war that resulted in the Israelites slaughter of the Benjaminites (man, woman, child and beast). Over 400,000 Israelites assembled to the Levite's call of war against the Benjaminites who had gathered a meager 25,700 men (Bible Gateway).

In 2 Samuel 13, the bible introduces rape by a family member. Amnon, the son of King David, lusts after his brother Absalom's sister, Tamar. Devising a plan and feigning sickness, Amnon ask David to send Tamar to him and take care of him. When Tamar brings him food, forlorn Amnon clears all servants from the room and asks Tamar to lie with him. When Tamar refuses, he rapes her. The result of the rape fills Amnon with hatred and he banishes Tamar from his home in disgrace.

When Tamar returns despondent to Absalom's home, Absalom asked if Amnon had lain with her and Tamar confesses to the rape. King David hearing about the rape, is furious with Amnon, but Absalom disguises his hatred towards his brother. He waits two years before he convinces David to allow his brother to accompany him to the sheepshearers. Once, there Absalom orders the King's sons to kill Amnon which they do. Absalom flees to Geshur for three years after the murder of his brother Amnon (Bible Gateway).

These biblical passages are clear—the rape is immediately acknowledged and believed. The victim is protected, the community is alerted, and the punishment is death. Although 75 percent of the United States identifies as Christian and consults biblical texts for guidance, America's current rape myths associated with victim blame and shame are not supported by the behaviors found within the Bible. Rape myth acceptance is a contradiction of the penalties and punishments enforced in the U.S. rape culture. The focal concerns for decision making regarding rape are quite different on the micro level (i.e., victims, offender, advocates, law enforcement) and the macro level of the social institutions (church, universities, courts) that are required to provide consequences that match the severity of the crime of sexual violence and rape. With a culture of victim blaming, and shaming, most victims won't report for fear that the perpetrator will not be prosecuted, or their credibility will be questioned (Bernsten, 2017). These viewpoints are reflected in America's historical punishments for sexual and rape offenses.

Sex Assault and Rape Sanctions in Colonial Times

Colonial times in America provided a definition for rape law (Bishop, 2018): "carnal knowledge of a woman 10 years or older, forcibly and against her will."

But the word rape (meaning to seize) was not used until it was associated with the "nigger rapist" (Conti, 2016). In colonial times, it was easier for the societal belief to exist that black men were more likely to violate white women due to the collective perception of their virility, political, social, and economic subjugation as a result of their enslavement (Block & Culture, 2006). For example, if you were a black slave and accused of the attempted rape or rape of a white women in 1819, judges in the southern state of Virginia believed it their obligation to exercise moral fortitude of taboos and fear of black male sexual aggression with castration (Bardaglio, 1994). Thomas Jefferson suggested castration as an acceptable rape punishment in the late 1700s (Block & Culture, 2006). Most historical rulings rarely dispensed this sanction to the dominant and powerful white males of colonial times. Applying the focal concerns theory to the subjugated class of the enslaved populace with limited agency, the first focal concern of offender blameworthiness is modified, and the intersection of status, race, and gender become significant factors for decisions regarding the crime of rape. If you were a person of color and enslaved, more dismal and dire circumstances would befall you if charged with rape and the sexual violation of another. For example, black males were easily assigned blame. The second focal concern of keeping the community safe became part of the social institutions of master and slave. A slave owner could kill his slave if he was accused of rape and the rape of white women would lead to swift law enforcement. Public lynching by townsmen or speedy trials in which the offender was imprisoned, were prosecuted more consistently (Block & Culture, 2006). Ironically, rape laws did not consider the possibility that children or men could be raped against their will. In court cases with men, these laws were considered "sodomy laws" and most abuses were associated with prisoners or slaves as victims of race, class and gender (Foster, 2011). For example, one of the earlier cases in the 1600s involved Nicholas Sension of Connecticut who was charged with the abuse of several of his servants. Yet, many colonial historians have neglected to discuss the sodomy abuses of enslaved male bodies as a result of ownership. A slave, Itanoka was repeatedly sexually assaulted by his overseer, Urban. Itanoka describes his abuser in the following terms: "Urban was described as a ravisher who, Itanoko explained, was "struck by my comeliness," and he did "violate, what is most sacred among men."

Sodomy was an acceptable punishment for captured prisoners (Foster, 2011). It was also reported that Native American prisoners were sodomized and sexually abused. Abolitionist accounts have reported the homosexual tendencies of white males during the domination of other males in order to control them with forced sex (Kitch, 2009). Subjugated tactics of the "feminization" of prisoners were utilized but also provided evidence of the support of social institutions use of rape to dehumanize and degrade captives. The laws of colonial times included the distinction between coerced sex and forced sex.

Coerced sex was considered consensual (Block & Culture, 2006). The court decisions of earlier centuries considered the intersection of patriarchy, social status, race, and economics as factors for judgments against perpetrators. In the case of Mary Jinkins of Maine, she accused her neighbor of attempted rape in 1710. Her neighbor—John White, knowing Mary's husband was out of town, visited her home with the intent to coerce Mary into sex. He sat most of the day talking to her, helped her put the kids to bed and bolted the door, alerting Mary of his sexual desires and intentions. After a prolonged struggle, Mary complied, and John spent the night leaving the home after Mary's mother arrived the next morning. Oddly, the courts punished both Mary and John with lewdness and fifteen lashes when the rape was brought to trial. Punishments in colonial times consisted of beatings or lashings with whips/cowhide, and several days in the stockade to encourage public shame and humiliation, dunking chairs, and fines. The focal concerns theory is aptly applied to this case. In this case, the offender's blameworthiness is weakened because the courts reduced the severity of the crime because the victim complied with the sex as a result of coercion. The focal concerns of keeping the community safe and the practical considerations and resources available for conviction and sentencing were minimal (Steffensmeier, Ulmer, & Kramer, 1998). It was not uncommon for courts to include moral judgments with rape prosecutions that may judge both the attacked and the accused. Such cases and punishments can be found with enslaved populations.

It was well known that enslaved women of color were seen as hypersexual and sexually exploited by their owners and others for breeding and forced sex. In 1855, Celia, a nineteen-year-old slave was repeatedly raped by her master, Robert Newsom, for five years before she killed him (Harris, 2017). Newsom purchased Celia when she was fourteen, and she gave birth to a child. Nevertheless, the courts did not seek mercy for Celia and chose to make an example out of her defiance by executing her for her crime. Slaves did not have recourse in the courts when they were victimized and acted out. Moreover, the focal concerns theory is applied to the offender's blameworthiness and the victim's limited agency. Because an enslaved women killed her owner, the intersection of power, status, race, and gender are noteworthy factors for further analysis.

Blameworthiness is reduced because of the status of the owner within the community. The courts are tasked with keeping the community safe. If Celia was absolved of her crime, it would threaten the power structure in three ways: status, gender, and race. A white slave owner's right to exploit the bodies of their slaves was an integral component of bondage (Klitch, 2009). It was not uncommon for enslaved women's bodies to be used for breeding. More important, to permit a slave to murder their white slave owner without consequence would subvert the regulation of the second focal concern: to keep the community safe. The social cost of the conviction provided a clear message to the community (owners and slaves) that slaves would be executed for killing their white owners. This was a pragmatic attempt to maintain order and stability among the enslaved and white populations. Enslaved men were also victims of sexual exploitation and there are many accounts of Black male slaves who were coerced by the "mistress" of the household to have sex (Foster, 2011).

It was reported that Mulatto or fair-skinned slaves were objects of desire for white women. For example, "fetish markets" existed throughout the antebellum south that displayed Mulatto slaves as sexual objects and exotic possessions. Slavery ensured that people of color did not own their bodies and were subjected to sexual objectification, degradation, exploitation, and violation from both white men and women. It is this history that can also be attributed to the societal perceptions of "the brute caricature" in which sociopathic, black males brutalized and raped white women against their will and were later hunted and lynched by angry white mobs seeking retribution. These distorted views perpetuated negative beliefs of the enslaved, the rape myth ideas of their immoral sexuality and sexual violations (Pilgrim, 2000) while reinforcing the social institutions (courts) normalization of inaction to prevent rape against people of color (Sailofsky, 2019).

In 1808 in New York, Sylvia Patterson, a free black woman raped by Captain Dunn, successfully charged a white man of significant power with rape. Although she won her case, during the trial, she was labeled hypersexed, promiscuous, and sexually diseased. While Dunn was found guilty of "assault with the intent to seduce," his punishment was a one dollar fine (Conti, 2016). When considering the intersection of race, gender, class inequalities, and rape in colonial times, many women, including women of color, could not seek legal justice or institute charges of rape without the help of the "male head of households." (Block & Culture, 2006). In most cases, male head of households could be identified as fathers, uncles, brothers, and cousins who were charged with caring for female relatives. But, if these males believed that a trial could be too lengthy, that his family may be humiliated and embarrassed by the accounting of the rape, or if they were the sexual predators, it was unlikely that female relatives would obtain justice in local courts for sexual violence. Using the focal concerns evaluation, there is a shift associated with the second and third focal concerns: community safety, social cost, and the consequence of the conviction. In the above-mentioned case, offender blameworthiness is not questioned. Dunn attempts to pay for his crime with a watch and liquor. Sylvia's husband refuses, however, the court is not concerned with the ability to keep the victim or the community safe, the second focal concern. Though found guilty, Captain Dunn's nefarious $1.00 fine is significantly lower than the initial proposal of the watch and liquor. More importantly, it is not a deterrent for future crimes. The third focal concern of social cost is problematic, because Dunn and deplorable men like him will not receive a sentence for their sexual violent crime. In this case, the victim is humiliated and labeled. Thus, the outcome does not match the crime and it sends a message to the townspeople that shame and humiliation of a black victim of rape is an acceptable practice. Yet, in cases where the victim is a white woman, we see a distinction within the focal concerns application.

When Frances Tomlinson was raped by her uncle, she initially did not tell anyone about the assault (Sneed, 2018). However, when her mother began to inquire about the peculiar nature of her brother-in-law's behavior (silence and keeping his distance from the family), Frances fully acknowledged that her uncle had sexually violated her. Frances's father was informed of the assault and sought justice from the courts. In 1803, Richard Tomlinson went on trial for the rape of his niece Frances in Kentucky. Yet, Frances was not allowed to testify against her uncle in court and was ordered (by her father) to stay with cousins out of town. After the trial, Richard approached his brother for leniency (which his brother did not provide), and the courts sentenced him to ten years in a Kentucky jail for the rape of his niece (Sneed, 2018). When white men were accused of sexual assault and rape violations, they often appealed to the head of the household to resolve the issue. However, in this case the focal concerns perspective was accurately applied. Richard's blameworthiness was not questioned, and his brother consulted the courts for justice. In order to keep Frances safe, her father did not permit her to testify or allow her to remain in town during the trial. Ridicule with blame and shame are not associated with this case and the community remains safe because Richard is sentenced to ten years in jail. He is no longer a threat to others thus reducing the social cost imposing a sentence that matches the crime. But Richard makes one final attempt to appeal to his brother for leniency in order to negotiate his prosecution. However, leniency is not granted, and the courts comply with an appropriate sentence.

Negotiations and Prosecutions

In the previously mentioned Patterson case, Captain Dunn attempted to give her husband a watch and purchase liquor to appease any objections (Block & Culture, 2006). Though unsuccessful, it was clear that powerful men believed they could negotiate their way out of a prosecution for sexual violence. If sexual assault transpired when a male head of household was not present, many women would wait until their return to seek local justice. In 1789, Rebecca Foster refused to seek justice when she was sexually violated until her husband came back from his trip. The intersection of class and gender are important social injustices to consider during colonial times. If a poor, lower-class female head of household was alerted that a sexual assault of her child or relative had occurred, she was reluctant to report the crime because she was intimidated and "did not wish the trouble" (Block & Culture, 2006). In colonial times, women did not feel empowered to report sexual assault. One reason may be associated with the treatment of accusers when reporting the attacks.

When two British soldiers gang raped Elizabeth Johnstone in 1776 in Newtown, Long Island, after illegally entering her home and threatening to kill her, the courts weren't kind to her (Block & Culture, 2006). The barrage of questions that she faced after the assault could have easily intimidated and discouraged Elizabeth from pursuing prosecution:

Was she certain that the men entered and emitted in her body? Was the attack done by force and against her consent? Did she resist with all of her power? How soon after the attack did she complain to officials? Did she have marks of violence on her body? Did she call for help as much as she could? How close was her nearest neighbor?

With several occupants of Elizabeth's house corroborating her assault, she was not deterred, and her attackers were prosecuted, court martialed, and sentenced to death by hanging. Each focal concern of offender blameworthiness, community safety, and practical social cost for sentencing were addressed. However, the treatment of rape victims in courts and the questioning of her actions during the violent assault set legal precedents that required further need for (a) the corroboration by witnesses and (b) circumstantial evidence. Men found the need to obtain evidence by inspecting an area where the sexual assault occurred, or soiled clothing, in the hopes of using the evidence found in an upcoming trial.

Such is the 1817 case when George Saub from Virginia examined the area of the field where his daughter claimed she was victimized and found evidence to substantiate her claims (Block & Culture, 2006). The field showed the place where the assault occurred and a "trampled ground." Men were needed for the crime of sexual assault to be prosecuted and brought to trial in the courts. These courts consisted of male lawyers, magistrates, male defendants, and male jurors. The intersection of power, status, and gender were illuminated with the limited agency that women possessed during trials. Women would face their attacker in court and provide statements that recounted the sexual assault. Discussing sexual violations in an open forum was frightening and scary for these courageous women that sought prosecution in earlier centuries. Ironically, the twentieth century sexual assault and rape cases provide similar cultural scripts previously associated with colonial prosecutions.

Twentieth Century Sexual Violence and Prosecutions

African American women were fighting a silent war against white men and sexual violence (Freedman, 2013). Portrayed as the jezebel, black women were associated with "lewd and promiscuous behavior and became targets for sexual violence (Pilgrim, The Jezebel Stereotype, 2002). Previous depictions of both black men and women were that black men were predators and "brutes" who pursued white women and black women were "less virtuous" and could be disrespected, fondled, harassed, and raped. During the Great Northern Migration, Ida B. Wells implored white men to respect black women (Freedman, 2012; Freedman, 2013). Segregation facilitated the continued subjugation of black men and women. If a black man was suspected of lewd behavior towards a white woman, public justice in the form of lynching was the punishment and the prosecution was death. If the accused survived the lynch mob and a trial followed, a conviction was certain. The intersection of race, gender and status was clearly defined within the courts. While social injustice for blacks was more likely in the court systems of the twentieth century, it did not stop African-Americans from pursuing justice in the convictions of sexual violent crimes. (Flood, 2012). But what's important to note, is the discrimination African American women often faced when dealing with the justice system setup to help them defend themselves against their attackers (Freedman E., 2013). If their attacker was black, they often remained silent because they did not want to be seen as another accuser of a black male. If, the attack was interracial, defense attorneys often sought to use racial derogatory statements that supported the "jezebel" mentality during a rape trial. Like the prosecutions from earlier decades, a black woman's objectification and promiscuity was part of the defense attorney's strategy that attributed to her ability to provide consent. The inability to prosecute white males for the sexually violent acts, made it difficult for black women to receive a fair trial. Jim Crow laws and the segregated climate aided sexual violence against black women. White privilege led to acquittals in rape cases or dismissals of charges that were rarely brought to trial. The focal concerns associated with sexual violence and black women were not applied when considering prosecutions. Offender blameworthiness was diminished and blaming the victim for sexual promiscuity enhanced (Steffensmeier, Ulmer, & Kramer, 1998). This negatively affected a victim's willingness to speak out against her attacker. Additionally, it interfered with a victim's decision-making ability to keep the community safe which also affected the third focal concern: the ability to obtain a conviction.

In 1944, while walking home from church, Recy Taylor was kidnapped, blindfolded, dragged into a car at gunpoint filled with six white men and taken to a wooded area in Abbeville, Alabama, and repeatedly raped. She spoke out about her kidnap and brutal gang rape, which resulted in alerting the sheriff of her rape, and his solution was to remain silent and not speak about the rape. Additionally, her home was firebombed, and her family (husband, daughter) moved to her father's home for safety. Taylor identified the car teenagers drove and one of her rapists to the sheriff (Biography, 2018). When the grand jury refused to indict the men accountable, the NAACP answered the public outcry, thus sending activist Rosa Park to investigate (Redden, 2017). Many prominent celebrities, W. E. B. DuBois and Langston Hughes came to Mrs. Taylor's defense imploring the Alabama governor to take action. The rapists made false statements saying that Taylor was previously jailed, had a venereal disease, yet justice alluded her and her rapists were acquitted of all charges. Rape culture impacts the United States not only at the individual level but also at the institutional level, affecting how victims are perceived and essentially how cultural systems treat them, including how law enforcement and police officers interact with victims.

Present Day Prosecutions

In the twentieth century and post-millennial era, most prosecutions and convictions of sex crimes are subjected to state and federal laws (Spohn & Holleran, 2004). When a sex crime is reported, the charges are recorded by local law enforcement and the prosecutors determine if the charges will be filed for indictments. There are several factors that determine prosecution. First, the prosecutors must consider the victim's "credibility, character, and behavior." Next, prosecutors are concerned with the odds of winning the case and will judge if the judge and jurors believe the victim's testimony of the events that resulted in the sexual assault or rape. Stereotypes associated with victimization are essential strategies used by prosecutors when presenting evidence of a sexual assault. A prosecutor may seek to corroborate the victim's account of the events through evidence such as rape kits and possible witnesses. However, in many cases of sexual assault, evidence and witnesses are not often available. When acquaintance or marital rape occurs, these convictions are harder to obtain because of the possibility of consent. Unfortunately, sex assaults or rapes from strangers have a higher rate of conviction because the victim does not have an established relationship with the predator. Gender, age, "blame and believability" factors are collected by local law enforcement and placed in the victim's file. These factors are associated with the moral factor of the victim that include possible criminal record, substance abuse, unwed mother, sexual activity history, or risk taking behaviors. During the reporting of the sex crime, police officers may ask if the victim was alone (walking home, using public transportation late at night, in a bar, club, or party). Answers to these questions have been associated with the reasons why local law enforcement agents won't test rape kits because they believe that the victim may be viewed as "culpable" by judges and jurors (Vagianos, 2017). Tying physical evidence to the sex crime is an important factor that prosecutors consider when contemplating charges against an offender, however, weapon usage is also an important variable considered in sexual violent crimes (Spohn & Holleran, 2004). While the rape reform laws from the 1970s ushered in the introduction of the rape advocate with rape counseling centers, medical and legal services for victims, changes to rape laws that considered males as victims and females as perpetrators, rape myths continue to exist among law enforcement officers (Page, 2010). In chapter two, the historical rape definitions used by the Department of Justice for convictions will be examined. Various forms of rape with penalties and associated statutes will also be investigated. Lastly, the application of the focal concerns theory with the denial, inaction, and information suppression (DIIS) theoretical perspective will be introduced.

CHAPTER TWO

~

How America Defines
Sexual Assault and Rape

The goal of this chapter is to introduce the denial, inaction, and information suppression theory (DIIS) of criminal justice institutions related to the submission and prioritization of sexual assault kits. Additionally, the antiquated definition of rape from the U.S. Department of Justice that existed until 2013 will be explored in order to establish the foundation for the rape culture within jurisdictions across America. The current backlog of sexual assault kits (SAKs) that languish in police storage across the United States has led to the denial of justice for countless victims of sexual violence (Valentine, et al. 2016; Campbell and Fehler-Cabral, 2018). There are approximately 200,000+ sexual assault kits that have not been tested, and some SAKs were collected thirty years ago (End the Backlog, 2019; Campbell et al., 2016). Much of the evidence collected was never sent to forensic labs for testing (justice denied), or SAKs were sent to forensic labs but were not tested due to limited resources (justice delayed) and attributed to the current backlog (Randol & Sanders, 2015; Campbell and Fehler-Cabral, 2018). Law enforcement agencies throughout numerous states have engaged in this practice of inaction while disregarding the possibility that the trace evidence collected (i.e. semen, saliva, hair samples, skin, etc.) from SAKs may lead to the potential prosecution of an offender and decrease the number of undetected rapists in our communities (Lisak and Miller 2002).

Lisak and Miller's (2002) findings (N=1,882) revealed that undetected rapists posed a colossal threat to the safety and security of our society because of the possibility of repeat offenses of sexual violence. Approximately 120 rapists were responsible for further acts (1,225) of interpersonal violence, and repeat rapists averaged 5.8 rapes each (Lisak & Miller, 2002; Lisak, 2006). Furthermore, it is equally important to test rape kits for DNA evidence because post-submissions may generate Combined DNA Index System (CODIS) matches (Campbell, Pierce, et al. 2016).

CODIS is a national database created and maintained by the FBI that can identify DNA matches of past offenders' felonious crimes and provide DNA hits to other cases. Once previously unsubmitted SAKs are tested, CODIS matches of DNA evidence linked to serial rapists have been identified. End the Backlog (2019) has identified three states in which countless serial rapists were found after forensic lab testing. Cleveland, Ohio submitted 13,931 SAKs and found 505 serial rapists; Detroit, Michigan submitted 11,137 SAKs and found "825 serial rapists while obtaining 215 convictions." Memphis, Tennessee submitted 12,162 SAKs that led to 2,612 investigations and requests for 270 indictments (End the Backlong, 2020). These convictions and indictments provide evidence of the importance of the submission of all SAKs for DNA analysis. The fact that statewide initiatives must be adopted in order to reform current policies and compel law enforcement agencies to submit all SAKs for forensic analysis is disturbing. Denial, inaction, and information suppression (DIIS) theory was developed in order to connect systemic inaction with pervasive attitudes and behaviors of criminal justice institutions (i.e., police, detectives, prosecutors, jurors, and judges) that prevent the fair and unbiased investigation and prosecutions of rape cases across America.

Denial, Inaction, and Information Suppression (DIIS) Theory

Detectives are the "gatekeepers" that make decisions to submit a SAK for DNA analysis (Hendrix, et al. 2020). Currently, law enforcement detectives and prosecutors use prioritization of SAKs in order to determine if valuable resources should be used to obtain DNA evidence for conviction (Campbell, Pierce, Sharma, Feeney & Fehler, 2016). Law enforcement prioritization of SAKs is determined by the victim-offender relationship (stranger vs. non-stranger), victim's credibility, victim's cooperation, and location of the sex assault. The national backlog has driven the U.S. Department of Justice (DOJ) with the Office on Violence Against Women (OVW) to develop the best practices to improve the response of law enforcement agencies associated with violent crimes against women (i.e., domestic violence, sex assaults/rapes) (U.S. Department of Justice Office on Violence Against Women, 2018). Estrich (1987) stated that law enforcement agencies make a distinction between real rape and simple rape. Real rape is a sexual assault committed by a stranger, gang rapes, and may include the use of weapons, and sexual violent acts without consent. A simple rape is a sexual assault committed by a non-stranger (i.e., family, spouse, friend, clergy, scout leader, co-worker, boyfriend, client, etc.), and some believe sex may include consent. Since 93 percent of sexual assaults are perpetrated by non-strangers, these definitions contribute to the bias of the seriousness of sexual assault which can result in victim-blaming and have led to few convictions for known sex offenders (Campbell & Fehler-Cabral, 2018).

If an investigator believed the rape was consensual, this bias affects a victim's credibility and will determine if a SAK is submitted for testing. However, with non-stranger rapes the identity of the offender is known, yet SAKs for non-strangers are submitted for DNA testing at a lower rate (Campbell, Pierce, Sharma, Feeney & Fehler, 2016). Non-strangers may be repeat offenders. Empirical evidence identified CODIS matches with approximately 59.1 percent of non-stranger cases receiving CODIS hits, while 40.9 percent of stranger cases received CODIS hits with stranger sex assaults (Campbell, Pierce, Sharma, Feeney & Fehler-Cabral, 2016). These CODIS hits can match offenders to additional felonies. If a sex offender's identity is known, but an investigator will not submit the rape kit for DNA evidence, there must be other factors preventing law enforcement agents from pursuing convictions.

Hendrix et al. (2020) sampled 321 law enforcement agencies and found that fewer than 60 percent of SAKs are submitted for testing and the factors associated with those submissions are not solely related to limited resources and staffing but the result of a culture of victim-blaming. More importantly, this study suggests that the understaffing and lack of resources available for thorough investigations for sexual violent crimes was attributed to a "lack of victim-centeredness, other attitudes and behaviors aimed at dismissing victims or SAKs." These widespread attitudes resulted in justice denied for victims of sexual violence and exhibit the inaction of criminal justice institutions to effectively investigate, prosecute, and convict sex offenders and predators. Failure to submit SAKs for forensic analysis results in the suppression of the information that can be obtained from the trace evidence collected. Moreover, if the evidence collected results in a CODIS hit and DNA match to a sex offender or predator, further investigation may lead to indictments and convictions. DIIS Theory masks the focal concerns initially addressed in chapter 1: (a) offender blameworthiness, (b) keeping society safe and (c) practical consequences and potential social costs (Steffensmeier, Ulmer and Kramer 1998).

Law enforcement agencies take an oath of policing "to protect and serve" the community. This is the second focal concern identified by Steffensmeier, Ulmer and Kramer (1998). However, the prioritization of rape kits in which rapes by strangers are more likely to be submitted to forensic labs supports the rape culture associated with judgments regarding victims' credibility and the cultural attitudes held by detectives (Campbell, Pierce, et al. 2016). When investigations are closed prematurely, sex offenders are not held accountable and less likely to be prosecuted. RAINN (2020) reports that five out of every one thousand rapists will be convicted and imprisoned. This affects the third focal concern that increases the societal cost when rapists and sexual predators escape prosecution and are free to commit new sex crimes and other felonious acts (Lisak and Miller 2002), but it can also be attributed to inaction, part of the DIIS theory. These jurisdictional cultural attitudes may be contributed to the antiquated rape definition used for decades to prosecute rapes.

In 2013, the federal guidelines for rape changed after the use of an eighty-year-old definition was abandoned and modified because it no longer fit America's current rape culture ideals. Today, rape is defined as: "penetration, no matter how slight, of the vagina or anus with any body part or object, or oral penetration by a sex organ of another person, without the consent of the victim" (Federal Bureau of Investigation Criminal Justice Information Services Division 2013).

Prior to the rape addendum, the old definition of rape included "The carnal knowledge of a female forcibly and against her will" (Federal Bureau of Investigations 2014). This definition did not account for other forms of rape that included children, males, (Coxell and King 2010) sexual minorities (LGBT) (Nelson, 2012; Sigurvinsdottir & Ullman, 2016); penetration with objects, unconscious and non-consenting victims thus making it difficult to accurately report forms of sexual violence and prosecute the predators (United States Department of Justice 2012).

While most of the mainstream discussions and ideas of rape culture are found on college campuses, America's rape culture is much more pervasive and normalized. The use of the eighty-year-old definition until 2013 showed that Americans were stuck in old standards and beliefs that did not support all human rights. The previous definition did not allow us to use the word rape when we learned that children were robbed of their sexual innocence by family members or acquaintances. Once, unconscious victims were not considered rape victims because the words "forcibly" was included in the older definition. Additionally, law enforcement did not consider that males were also survivors of rape (Lara and Meyer 2014). A National Crime Victimization Survey (2013) reported that 46 percent of males experienced sexual victimization by a female perpetrator, and 89 percent of juvenile boys reported sexual abuse from female staff. These antiquated definitions did not consider the fact that a male could be a victim of sexual violence (Federal Bureau of Investigation Criminal Justice Information Services Division 2013). National surveys conducted by the federal government (i.e., Centers for Disease Control and Prevention, Bureau of Justice Statistics, Federal Bureau of Investigation), considered the stereotypical paradigm that sexual violence was a women's issue or that the perpetrator was more likely to be male. Archaic definitions have prevented the accurate reporting of sexual victimization of both men and women. It has also contributed to the underreporting of sexual minorities of the LGBT communities.

In a 2015 study of college students (N=10, 646), bisexual women or those who identified themselves with newer terms (i.e., non-binary, pansexual, or queer) experienced the highest rates of sexual victimization as well as gay and transgender males (Eisenberg et al, 2017; Coulter & Rankin, 2017). Using the Online College Social Life Survey (OCSLS), a cross-sectional survey of 21,000 students, Ford and Soto-Marquez (2016) reported that "one in every four gay and bisexual men reported similar rates of sexual assault as heterosexual women." Moreover, two of five bisexual women had experienced sexual assault as undergraduates thus making this population more vulnerable than other sexual minority groups.

The change in the definition of rape and modified addendum was necessary to support the dominant nomenclature and inclusive statistical reporting that incorporated the intersections of (gender, age, and sexual orientation). The accurate reporting of sexual violence is not enough to eradicate sexual violence in the United States. For example, in 2017, the FBI reported rape statistics from 2016 to be 95,730 while murders were 17,250 for the same year (Federal Bureau of Investigations 2017). This meaning suggests that a person is approximately six times more likely to be raped than murdered in America. A dismal reality.

If Americans hope to see a decline and future end to its rape culture, it must be proactive in changing the rape myth perceptions of the societal beliefs of rape. Additionally, it must create campaigns that encourage rape victims to report their experiences, extend the statutes of limitations terms for victim reporting, increase mandatory minimums (statewide) for the prosecutions of rape, and enhance social programs that provide empathetic training for law enforcement and the community that teach loving and caring responses to victimization.

So, what acts can be defined as rape? Based on the federal guidelines implemented in 2013 by the Federal Bureau of Investigation, children are the most vulnerable population that should be considered when defining rape. One reason for their vulnerability is their dependence on another person for their safety and protection. They are left alone under the care of the perpetrator or are taken to places (homes, extra-curricular activities, social events, etc.) where sexual violence can happen. Additionally, they are small in size and stature. They aren't strong enough to fight off a predator that is bigger than them and do not possess the intellectual capacity to understand what sex is, provide consent, or comprehend the violation (Tracy 2016). Rape by a family member helps explain the role of dependency.

Types of Sexual Violence

With *incest rape*, children and teens are vulnerable victims of parents, siblings, and relatives (aunt, uncles, cousins) and forcibly raped. The process may begin as touching, caressing, and fondling that escalates to sexual intercourse. Depending on the age of the child when sex is first initiated, the violation can easily affect the child's future ideas of the act of sex, his/her sexual identity, and the development of mental health issues (Pullman 2017). More importantly, if left unchecked or less severe consequences are imposed on the predator, the incest of children may last for years and continue into adolescence and adulthood thus altering the sexual response of the individual (Middleton 2013).

In one case, Becca was repeatedly molested, raped, and physically abused by her father, Ruben, throughout her childhood only to become pregnant with his child at the age of fifteen (Slusser 2015). Though school officials reported Ruben to Child Protective Services after Becca recounted the details of her life, Child Protective Services (CPS)'s intervention did not deter Ruben's continued abuse of his daughter, Becca. It is not uncommon that sex abuse of a minor continues after a CPS investigation (A Better Childhood 2020). This is the second and third stage of DIIS theory known as inaction and information suppression. The CPS investigation and follow-up would require Becca to be removed from her home. But this did not happen.

Each year, there are countless reports of child sexual abuse with CPS investigations, but many reports are erroneously unfounded; the CPS follow-up to the claim of abuse is delayed or completely ignored thus supporting institutional inaction (A Better Childhood 2020). When this happens, children remain in the home with the abuser, or children are removed from the home and placed in the government foster care system. For Becca, the abuse continued, and after she gave birth to her new baby, Rowena, Ruben continued the intergenerational physical and sexual abuse of Rowena that began at age one and ended at age ten. Eventually, Becca and Rowena escaped their abusive father with the help of their older sister, Rachel, but Rowena would later be abused by her stepfather (Becca's new husband) and become pregnant by him but suffer a miscarriage. Rowena is truly a rape survivor because as she states "she survived the sexual assault and rape of her biological father, uncle, half-brother, step-father and other men." (Slusser 2015). Rowena and Becca's fate of intergenerational sexual abuse may have been very different if a follow-up visit from CPS would have occurred and Becca was removed from the home.

The underreporting of the sexual abuse of a child is one of the barriers to ending it, but the alternative to remaining in the home with an offender is government provided foster care. The child welfare system is not often the best alternative for children and teens seeking refuge from sexual abuse. According to the The Children's Bureau of Statistics (2018), there are 676,000 that were victims of abuse or neglect with 687,345 children in foster care. But the government facilities or foster care often ignore additional abuse of children and teens within the child welfare system (A Better Childhood 2020). "They often are terrorized sexually, physically or emotionally while under the states' care." With 20 percent of the child abuse cases occurring before the age of eight (Darkness to Light n.d.), it is paramount that we create solutions that inform our children about their bodies and potential abuse violations at earlier ages. Additionally, we must adopt laws that effectively prosecute the non-stranger offenders and provide resources and services for the victims earlier in order to end the cycle of sexual abuse thus stamping out future abuse in the survivor's life. Chapter 3 will explore the Fail to Protect laws associated with children and teens sexual abuse. Next is *acquaintance rape*, which affects all groups: children, adolescents, college youth, and adults.

Also known as date rape, acquaintance rape is such an egregious act that 66 percent of reported rapes are associated with it (Tracy 2016). It's known as a problematic form of rape because the abuser and the abused often don't recognize the violation as rape because of the previously established relationship. For children and adolescents, the sexual abuse threat comes from babysitters, nannies, priests, teachers, coaches, community leaders, friends (often peers), and others. With sexually victimized children under the age of twelve, the law recognizes this act as *statutory rape*; however, this may also be correlated with age of consent laws for sexual activities (twelve to eighteen years old) that vary statewide (Tracy 2016). It is a crime to have sex with children and adolescents, although they may be old enough to provide consent for sex. The states dictate the enforcement of these laws because of the age of the two engaging in sex (same age) and the potential vulnerability of the youth who have sex with adults (Volokh 2015). At the time of the writing of this book, a case that would be considered statutory rape based on current and past laws has recently surfaced in the media.

Roy Moore, the 2017 Republican senate nominee, was accused of a 1979 sexual assault by a woman that was then fourteen years old (McCrummen, Reinhard and Crites 2017). Leigh Corfman says Moore, then a thirty-two-year-old assistant district attorney, befriended her mother outside an Alabama courtroom in Etowah County before her custody hearing. He asked to take care of the fourteen-year-old Leigh while her mother attended court. During his time with Leigh, he gave her his phone number and several days later, picked her up two blocks from her home. He then drove thirty miles to his home in the woods and kissed her for the first time. On a second visit, he removed her and his clothes, fondled her breasts over her bra, touched her inappropriately over her pants, and pushed her hand over his underwear. She wanted the ordeal to end, and she asked that Mr. Moore take her home. At the time, the age of consent laws in Alabama was sixteen years old. Leigh was two years shy of the age requirement.

She later reported the incident to two friends stating that she was seeing an older man. However, she did not report the sexual assault to her mother until the 1990s, when Roy Moore sought higher political office in Alabama. New allegations of eight additional accusers have surfaced in the Roy Moore case. Moore continues to deny the allegations, and it is not uncommon for high profile and powerful men to adopt the behaviors associated with DIIS theory: denial, inaction, and information suppression. This behavior is also associated with focal concerns of offender blameworthiness. In 2020, Roy Moore sought an Alabama senate seat but lost. To date, he was not investigated for sexual misconduct based on previous allegations.

Acquaintance rape can start as friendships but cross the line of consent and forcible rape. The abuser may believe that their friend may have encouraged the rape through certain actions. Additionally, the abused may have initially agreed to have sex, but later rescinded consent. With the victim assuming that he/she may have displayed "mixed signals," the feelings of self-blame and shame are the result of the violation (Weiss 2013). Abigail Hauslohner, a Washington Post Bureau Chief, recounts her story of rape from a longtime friend who invited her to his college for the weekend in order to attend a "real college party" hosted by his fraternity. Though she stated she lived with parents that had strict rules, they did not perceive her longtime friend to be a threat when they allowed her to visit his college.

After arrival at the frat party, he began plying her with drinks in which she slowly began to lose consciousness and found herself in a stranger's car.

She was later taken to her friend's dorm room where she would later be forcibly raped after repeated attempts to get her abuser to stop and repeatedly using the word NO! (Hauslohner 2014). She could not force him to stop because she had no control of her body. She explains that her body felt foreign and immobile, and her reactions slowed. Later, when she awoke from an unconscious stupor and in her friend's t-shirt, she did not know how the night had ended and immediately felt the need to vomit. When she was fully conscious, she asked that her friend take her home, riding silently in the car and vomiting again along the way. Once home, she sought refuge in her bedroom but did not tell her parents about the sexual assault. Although, she would report the rape to a mutual friend of the rapist a week later, Ms. Hauslohner's account of the rape was not validated because the mutual friend did not believe the "boy next door" would do something so frightening. With this example, the focal concern of offender blameworthiness and the first stage of denial from the DIIS theory would influence Ms. Hauslohner's decision to report the rape and would result in the second and third stages of inaction and information suppression. Apprehension to report the rape to law enforcement results in inaction and any information from the crime (i.e., identity of offender, DNA evidence, events of the crime) will not be shared with the community. But it is also associated with a victim's belief that her story is not credible based on stereotypes and labels as a result of her actions (i.e., drinking, partying, staying in her friend's frat room) (Campbell, Pierce, et al. 2016; Valentine et al., 2016). The incident was never reported to law enforcement, and it would take another year before Ms. Hauslohner would talk to a psychologist after a serious bout with depression. She would never see her abuser again, and he would be considered an undetected rapist (Lisak, 2008).

Predators may spend time "courting and grooming" their potential victims with special treatment, gifts, special friendships, special attention, and secret keeping in order to obtain consent. Gifts may be in the form of promotions or new job contacts, but it's important to note that for the predator, acquaintance rape is more about the ability to control the sexual interaction; and the abuser may hold the belief that the act is not considered rape (Edwards 2014). Non-consensual rape is often paired with acquaintance rape when drugs and alcohol are used, and the victim is often overpowered or worse—unconscious (Tracy 2016). With Abigail Hauslohner, she was a victim of date and nonconsensual rape.

For predators, drugs and alcohol are the perfect tool for unsuspecting victims. Drugs can easily be added to the punch bowl at a party or a drink at the club in order to reduce awareness of surroundings and coax a person into a room, bathroom stall, secluded place, or car. While the date rape drug, rohypnol, is well known (Donovan 2016) benzodiazapines and sedatives can easily be substituted in order to make a person vulnerable and amenable to sexual violence. When paired with alcohol, victims may not be able to recall events while unconscious, thus making the reporting of rape harder. Abigail Hauslohner (2014) believes she was victimized with the pairing of drugs and alcohol as the cause of her unconsciousness.

Alcohol depresses the central nervous system, and while the other drugs may be often discussed, it is alcohol that is easily accessible, and the "most dangerous" date rape drug associated with non-consensual victims (Grimes 2014). Gilmore, Lewis & George (2015) state that alcohol usage and sexual assault co-occur in 50-70 percent of sexual assaults. Some of these acts can be extremely violent, especially when the predator uses weapons, brute force, and assault to overpower the victim during the sexually abusive struggle. Some victims recognize that the rape can become more violent, so they acquiesce in order to reduce the amount of harm that may be inflicted on them. They stop struggling in the hopes that the abuser will finish quickly and they may get away safely. When nonconsensual rape is coupled with *aggravated rape*, we are introduced to more violent forms of rape perpetrated by strangers, partners, friends, and family (Tracy 2016). Associated with threats of physical harm or death, aggravated rape is extremely traumatic for the victim. The intimate sexual violation may be secondary to the beating and abusive assault the criminal inflicts on the helpless. The abused is in a fight for survival while hoping to fight off their attacker, reduce their vulnerability and rescind access to their body. Gabrielle Union, a Hollywood actress, has a unique survivor story of non-consensual and aggravated assault when she was raped, at gunpoint, in the back of a Payless Shoe Store (Union 2016). She was a sophomore in college working at the store when the rape occurred and has openly discussed the trauma of surviving the rape.

The result of the rape took a toll on her mental psyche associated with her belief that she was damaged. And yet Gabrielle Union was more fortunate than most survivors of aggravated and nonconsensual rape because her attacker was caught and prosecuted. Her rapist plead guilty and received a plea deal for thirty-three years (Saad 2017). However, over the year, while the rape trial proceedings took place, Gabrielle Union sought refuge in her home battling fear, guilt, coupled with shame and became a recluse.

Psychologically imprisoned in her home, she only left the sanctuary of it to attend therapy and the court hearings. Her case is a prime example of how the trauma of rape can rob your spirit, your identity, and strong sense of self years after the rape has occurred.

For children and adolescents that have long-term aggravated rape histories, the levels of sexual, physical, and emotional abuse may seem endless,
and they may adopt learned helplessness. A surrendering to the fact that
rape is the norm, and they can't do anything to protect themselves from
the repeated acts of violation and violence is a debilitating thought. *Partner
rape* can also follow a similar trajectory as the previously discussed forms of
rape. However, many people don't believe that partner rape (also known as
marital or spousal rape) exists (Basu 2015).

Special counsel to President Donald Trump and his long-time attorney,
Michael Cohen, defended Donald Trump against spousal rape accusations
from his ex-wife Ivana made in a 1989 deposition. Cohen stated that "by
definition, you can't rape your wife. He was incorrect because New York
state prohibited spousal abuse in 1984. But don't be fooled, for the victims
that suffer the forced and battery of bodily injuries from the person that is
supposed to love, honor, and cherish them; this destructive act erodes the
foundation of the marriage.

It snatches the self-esteem of the abused while empowering the spouse
to engage in more criminal violations in the future (Boardman 2015). It
becomes a guide that can be used to control, manipulate, and shame the
powerless to abide by every command inside and outside the bedroom (Allen
2015). In the case of Mandy Boardman, she knows how the repeated victimization by her husband can be nonconsensual and wreck the framework that
her marriage was built upon.

While she slept, her husband would dissolve Xanax or Ambien pills and
insert the cloudy liquid into her mouth in order to rape her. Passed out and
incapacitated, he would record them having sex on his phone (Boardman
2015). Mandy began to experience memory issues with tiredness and often
awoke with undissolved pills in her mouth that she couldn't explain. She
would be completely oblivious to the fact that her husband was drugging her
in order to have sex with her if she hadn't awakened one night to a flashlight
being shined in her face and her husband trying to conceal something in his
hand. Seeing him hide something between the mattress, she searched for the
item and found a pill filled with a cloudy like substance. Physically confront-
ing him, she demanded to know its contents. While he admitted his betrayal
and deceit, he promised he would stop, but he lied. As the years went by,
he continued to drug her, putting the liquid in her soda can and although
she knew they were growing apart and what he was capable of doing, she
was powerless (Guerra 2014). Additionally, she was "disgusted, confused,
and afraid" that he had manipulated her while she was in a coma like sleep.
Keeping a copy of the videos, she finally realized that her husband was raping

her and later divorced him. But she did not initially turn him into the police until she realized that her daughter could potentially be victimized by her father if left alone with him.

Divorce and sharing custody of the kids provided the perfect environment for abuse of her daughter to happen. She was mortified, and with the urging and support from her friend, she finally turned in the video to local law enforcement and criminally charged her ex-husband for rape. Over three years of court proceedings, David Wise was convicted of six Class B felonies which included rape and deviant conduct (Guerra 2014).

And while marital rape is criminalized nationwide, there are some limitations to the enforcement of the law in eight states. Allen (2015) explains that it is estimated that approximately 10-34 percent of intimate partnerships and marriages have occurrences of marital rape. Regardless of the definitions of rape provided by state and federal governments, the societal views in association with the reporting, law enforcement, and prosecution of the act should be more consistent. Special circumstances and limitations should not be assigned to its criminality. As a country, we should stand together as one to defeat the labeling of stigmas and fight to put an end to all forms of rape. More important, better mental health programs should be established to end the long suffering of those most affected by the act of rape: its survivors and its predators. Chapter three will focus on the sexual assault and rape of children and the types of offenders that engage in sexual abuse of minors. In addition, it will continue to explore the focal concerns of offender blameworthiness, keeping the community safe, and the practical and social costs that can prevent conviction and prosecution. Furthermore, DIIS theory will be applied in order to establish a connection between trusted social institutions that include (a) school: Chicago Public School District; (b) scouts: Boy Scouts of America; and (c) religion: Catholic Church that use denial, inaction, and information suppression that perpetuates sexual violence against the most vulnerable population: children.

CHAPTER THREE

~

Vulnerable Children Targeted for Sexual Violence

One of the most vulnerable populations affected by sexual violent crimes are children and teens. According to The Rape, Abuse & Incest National Network (RAINN, 2020), the statistics for sexual assault and rape are heartbreaking and staggering. Approximately one in four girls and one in six boys will be sexually assaulted before their eighteenth birthday. Within the United States, Child Protective Services (CPS) substantiates a sex abuse claim in which a minor is a victim every nine minutes. Child sexual abuse is defined as "a form of child abuse that includes sexual activity with a minor. A child cannot consent to any form of sexual activity" (RAINN,2020).

It was estimated that 93 percent of these minors know their abuser. Approximately 66 percent are ages twelve to seventeen and 34 percent are under twelve years old while 82 percent of these victims are female (RAINN, 2020). The numbers don't lie and paint a stark picture of the perplexing problem faced by many families. In order to address this issue, our local communities must be aware of the various ways a minor can be groomed, forced, and/or coerced to engage in inappropriate sexual activities. Currently, most solutions provide reactionary responses to this long-standing social problem. New solutions should be proactive and preventative. To continue to address the problem with old methods created from stereotypical social stigmas is to ignore the facts that these intimate violations greatly affect the future identity of two of the most vulnerable populations: children and teens. Parents are expected to educate their children about the potential for child sexual abuse (CSA), however, they may focus on strangers while the majority of CSA victims know their abuser (Deblinger, Thakkar-Kolar, Berry, & Schroeder, 2010). It is vital that parents, caregivers, family members, advocates, government, and social institutions interested in the safety of these minors and the reduction of these statistics learn more about predatory grooming methods.

The goal of this chapter is to identify the types of sex offenders and predators that target youth and the grooming factors associated with different levels of power and control utilized with predation. Additionally, denial, inaction, and information suppression (DIIS) theory in conjunction with the focal concerns theory of an offender's blameworthiness, keeping the community safe, and the practical and social costs that can prevent conviction and prosecution of sex offenders will be applied to the social institutions (Boys Scouts of America (BSA), the Catholic Church and the Chicago Public School) that engaged in the systemic sexual abuse of minors. Last, interviews from adult narratives will be incorporated to provide the raw data of oral histories of the unreported lived experience of children sexually groomed by manipulative youths and adults. These recollections may be triggering as a result of the graphic details; however, the survivors chose to provide an authentic factual account of the persistent child abuse of their past.

Predatory Adults Use of Power, Control, and Grooming

According to Young (1997) the hierarchical structure found in most households and lifestyles place the adult in power and the child in a subservient submissive role. Children and teens are taught to be obedient and respectful to their elders and to limit their objections when adults do things that they don't like. These social scripts of dependency that children are subjected, makes it hard for them to be cognitively and emotionally equipped to combat sexual manipulation from adults. The normalcy of intimate touch scenarios that children share with their parents and other caregivers require further exploration. A child is hugged, kissed, caressed, bathed, and clothed by adults. Additionally, youth learn the moral and cultural beliefs systems from significant adults in the form of child-rearing with the use of rewards and punishments thus fostering the education of appropriate norms within a household. However, children's dependency and sole reliance can lead to sexual exploitation from adults that are responsible for their care. Babysitters, coaches, and other mentors can engage in the sexual coercion and exploitation of minors because naive parents and family members trust them to participate in unsupervised visits with their unsuspecting child. There are various types of sex offenders and predators classified by the Office of Sex

Offender Sentencing, Monitoring, Apprehending, Registering, and Tracking (SMART) (Simons, 2020).

Child Sex Abuse: Defined

Child sex abuse can be defined as the use coercion or force to engage in sexual behaviors with children under the age of thirteen or when there is a five-year age difference between of a perpetrator the victim (Finkelhor, 1984). If the victim is between the ages of thirteen to sixteen and the perpetrator is at least ten years older than the victim. Coercion can be linked to the manipulation of the child to engage in touching or fondling of private areas of the body that may arouse the child. These sexual acts can be indirect or direct threats associated with secret keeping and grooming. The targeting of the child is based on the limited social interactions or position the child has within his/her social network. The limited social agency of the child is one of the factors recognized in targeting a victim. Perpetrators believe that the sexual relationship with the child is reciprocated and mutual (Simons, 2020).

Grooming

When children experience sexual violence at young ages, it is not uncommon for the abuse to happen over a period of time as a result of the sexual grooming process (Pollack, 2015). This process happens in stages so that the predator can have control over the setting and the psyche of the child. Ideally, the offender must have access and isolate the child to build trust. Unsuspecting parents must allow opportunities for the child to spend time alone with the abuser without interruption. Before the stage of sexual exploitation can be solidified, trust must be established between predator and child (Rufo, 2011). Like a stalker, the predator studies the child and learns his/her needs over an extended period of time. A neglected child, often ignored by parents can be easy to "befriend." Trust can be built through the expression of affection, praise, attention, and gift-giving to a vulnerable child. But it can also be established by becoming the confidante or keeper of the child's secrets. Giving advice, aid, protection, or serving as a surrogate parent or mentor help establish a "psychological hold on the child's mind that an offender is safe. This process takes time and once the child feels safe and secure, the predator moves to touching (Robertiello & Terry, 2007). Harmless tickling, bathing, or brushing fingers against genital regions and private parts can escalate to inappropriate touch and is deliberate and intentional behaviors that encourage compliance from the child victims. Each occurrence goes a little further than the previous attempts. This can best be described as "deceptive trust" and touch (Rufo, 2011). These sexual advances may also include rough and tumble play, watching a child undress, or exposure to pornographic images so that the predator can gauge the compliance of the child or teen when touched inappropriately. If the child does not reject the intimate touch and fails to establish a boundary, then the predator will assume, he/she can increase their sexual advances until boundaries are established (if, at all). This could be considered sexual seductive play that includes verbal, emotional, physical coercion, manipulation and incentives (Robertiello & Terry, 2007). Sexual exploitation can also take the form of sex education where the predator uses intimate touch to teach a child about sex and his/her body. For most children, this is their first sexual experience and if the child is aroused by the experience, it becomes the typical interaction between predator and child or a sexual game played. It will also become the measurement that abused children will use to evaluate new sexual experiences and their sexual self-concept. The sexual self-concept is best explained by the youth's perceptions of his/her sexual well-being. After abuse, positive perceptions of sexual self-esteem may be distorted by their earlier sexual experiences with predators (Scales Rostosky, Dekhtyar, Cupp, & Anderman, 2016). However, not all predatory forms of sexual abuse are gentle; some are sexually aggressive and violent. All sexually abusive encounters require secret keeping and the child is coerced into keeping the encounters quiet and hidden from others (Rufo, 2011). Some may use threats or additional gifts, but others may use alcohol and drugs to gain consent. When abusers are close in age to their victims, violence and physical abuse can be used. However, all will seek isolation and require the maintenance of secrecy. Once a child or teen is exposed to these negative sexual experiences, sexual risk-taking behaviors may increase with emotional anxiety, depression, and feeling of sexual inadequacy, as well as sexual preoccupations with sexual orientation and identity. Sexual self-efficacy is threatened. This is best defined as a child or teen's inability to control the intrusive sexual activity and situation (Scales Rostosky, Dekhtyar, Cupp, & Anderman, 2016). Children and teens may be unable to comprehend the sexual assault and the loss of their access to their body. Depending on the age and maturity level of the child or teen, they are unable to provide consent to the assault and may be overpowered by the perpetrator. In many cases, the minor is restrained, "held down" or restricted from movement due to the imposing physical stature of the abuser. Their genital regions of their bodies are violated when molested and/or penetrated. Psychologically, these youth experience the fight, flight, or shock activated by the neurobiological response system that may cause a child or teen to "freeze" during the traumatic assault (Thompson, Hannan, & Miron, 2014). Sexual assault victims are more likely to freeze during the sexual violation and become immobile. Reasons include fear from the traumatic violation, the realization that a trusted family member, or friend is causing harm, and the loss of control and power over one's body thus resulting the aforementioned immobilization. If they struggle to break free, the abuser may become more aggressive, intensify their restraint, and physically assault the child or teen (Ramirez, Jeglic, & Calkins, 2015). Thompson, Hannan, & Miron (2014) further state that repeated victimization increases emotional dysfunction and the influence of shame and guilt which are the psychological remnants of trauma affecting these victims. Once a youth becomes a victim of sexual violence, their ability to discern positive outcomes from future sexual experiences declines, thus negatively affecting their sexual self-efficacy (Scales Rostosky, Dekhtyar, Cupp, & Anderman, 2016). Other factors affecting a victims' sexual self-efficacy can be the reactions of the people who learn of the sexual assault. If a youth is blamed, shamed, guilted, ridiculed, or punished after revealing that he/she was a victim of a sexual assault, it is not uncommon for the victim to adopt low self-esteem (Kaukinen & DeMaris, 2005) Additionally, sexualized risk taking behaviors and distorted perceptions regarding sexual experiences may be present (Finkelhor, Ormrod, & Turner, 2007; Finkelhor, Shattuck, et al., 2014). This can be attributed to denial, inaction, and information suppression (DIIS) theory which will be discussed in below.

Denial, Inaction, and Information Suppression (DIIS) Theory

Denial, inaction, and information suppression theory can also be easily applied to the psyche of the victims during the molestation and sexual abuse acts. When a child or prepubescent teen is victimized by an adult, they feel powerless to the sexual assault (Lahav, Ginzburg, & Spiegel, 2019). The perpetrator has power and control over the child or teen's body and is often physically imposing and dominant. The powerlessness and loss of control linked with the freeze response of immobility and shock previously explained is associated with the ways a child "denies" their ability to control or comprehend the sexual violation of their body by a trusted friend or family member. Psychologically, the youth may dissociate from their body when experiencing pain and injury from the unwanted penetration of their genital regions (i.e., anus, vagina) (World Health Organization, 2003). This creates a numbness and a detachment from the emotional responses, thoughts, and sensations experienced by the body (Lahav, Ginzburg, & Spiegel, 2019). Memories, identity, and consciousness of the sexual violation can be repressed and if the child experiences repeated abuse, they continue to deny the ability to control the sexual assault. This first stage of denial of control can also be allied with the suppression of the events that leads to further denial of the sexual assault to others and maintenance of secrecy (O'Donohue, Benuto, Fondren, Tolle, & Vijay, 2013). According to Roland Summit, the child sexual abuse accommodation syndrome (CSAAS) can explain some abused child responses. Victims learn to accept their abuse, attempt to survive the guilt, shame of the sexual violations, and trust broken that they were helpless to control. Summit defines CSAAS with five stages: secrecy, helplessness, accommodation with entrapment, delayed disclosure, and retraction. The second stage of inaction is adopted by the child as a result of the demand of secrecy from the abuser either from fear as the result of threats or the belief of helplessness and the acceptance of the harm and pain caused from the sexual assault. Perpetrators may coerce with threats or provide gifts in order to maintain secrecy and the potential for future sex assaults (Pollack, 2015). Information regarding the assault is suppressed and hidden from others by both the abuser and the abused.

Incest: When the Sex Offender is a Relative

If the abuser is a relative, the child will not report the abuse because of cognitive dissonance (Buchbinder & Sinay, 2020). They know it's wrong, but children may not want harm, trouble, or incarceration to befall their relative (i.e., parent, sibling, uncle) and may withhold information to avoid the shame of other people (i.e., family members, friends, neighbors) learning about the sexual abuse. Children may be fearful that their victimization will not be believed, and they may lose the love and support of the other family members (Gqgabi & Smit, 2019). Yet, others believe that they will be physically harmed and victims of domestic violence. They worry that the family may be separated or split-up once law enforcement learns about the crime. Some continue to love their parent or relative although they are abusive and simply want the victimization to end. Young children have not formed the cognitive maturity to understand the complexities of their decision to tell the secret thus causing confusion and befuddlement. Self-blame is a factor that can delay truth telling (Okur, Pereda, Van, & Bogaerts, 2019). Some question—Why me—why was I chosen?

When sex offenders select their targets based on their vulnerabilities. These include children from single parent homes, females, foster care, stepchildren, impoverished, previous abuse (physical, sexual), isolated, neglected, or withdrawn children (World Health Organization, 2003). According to Groth (1979), each abuser has various typologies which helps identify the types of children and teens they may target for future sexual assaults. The next section of this chapter identifies the classifications of offenders while using oral narratives that provide the raw data and life experiences of survivors of childhood sexual abuse.

Child Sex Abusers and Perpetrators

Child sex abusers are not novel or typical. They can come from various demographics which include gender, status (economic, marital), race, ethnicity, and sexual orientation (Simons, 2020). Abusers may possess "poor social skills, feelings of inadequacy, loneliness, and sexual problems" (Groth, 1979; Simons, 2020). Most will normalize their sexual activities with children and are labeled as fixated because of their need to interact with children in order to fulfill their sexual desires. The majority of fixated child abusers select male victims and most likely have a history of sexual victimization (Perillo, Mercado, & Terry, 2008). Examples of fixated abusers include the Catholic Priests or Boy Scout Leaders (Mercado, Tallon, & Terry, 2008). Yet there are regressed child sex abusers that engage in sexual relationships with peers but various situational factors (loss of partner) or emotional distress can lead them to regress to sex with minors (Simons, 2020). Incest and female adolescents are the likeliest targets of the regressed sex abuser (Mercado, Tallon, & Terry, 2008). However, fixated sex abusers are more likely to engage in extrafamilial victimization and are labeled with pedophilia (Simons, 2020). Researchers are unable to identify one significant factor that can determine if an individual will sexually victimize a child. Although past childhood victimization is a known cause, other factors include (van den Berg, et al., 2020) :

1. Limited sexual sex regulation
2. Anti-social factors
3. Impulsivity
4. Genetic anomalies which included higher prenatal androgen levels, low testosterone levels and functionality associated with recidivism (Kruger, et al., 2019)

In one study that included 3,674 clerics, the characteristics and patterns of persistent offenders were investigated.

Diocesan clerics that had ten or more victims were compared to those that had (a) single, (b) moderate (two to three), or high (four to nine) (Mercado, Tallon, & Terry, 2008). Persistent child sex abuse was defined as clerics who were classified as fixated while regressed child sex abusers were more likely to engage in grooming behaviors that included relationships with the victims' families, providing or offering gifts for invasive (oral, vaginal, or anal penetration) or contact offenses (touching over/below clothing), and no contact offenses (photographs, pornography, verbal harassment). The age of the offender was significant because clerics that were young (thirty years of age) when the first offense occurred, were more likely to have a larger number of victims and engaged in child abusing activities for approximately eighteen years or more. Those with one victim were more likely to abuse a female, however, the majority of clerics were more likely to abuse male victims. However, denial, inaction, and information suppression can be identified based on the findings from this study. If a cleric abused one minor, 4 percent were reprimanded and returned to service, while approximately 36 percent of clerics that abused children between four and ten or more minors were reprimanded and returned to service. This supports the denial and inaction of social institutions like the diocese to hold clerics accountable for child sex abuse. In 33 percent of the cases, the diocese did not take action. Furthermore, there were few convictions of clerics and although 17 percent to 22 percent of police investigated cases of clerics that victimized a single or multiple number of minors, only 3 percent to 9 percent of clerics were convicted. These statistics support the idea associated with the focal concerns theory of offender blameworthiness, protecting the community and the practical and social costs of convictions. When assessing offender's blameworthiness, the demographics are considered which include age, race, sex, profession, and status which include societal stereotypes. Clerics are often white males that are hold iconic status in their community (McDowell, 2015). They are considered the physical personification of Christ, righteous, and virtuous. With the intersection of pious stereotypes, gender, and status, the offender blameworthiness of a revered priest of the community is unlikely.

Boys and Sex Abuse

With one of ten males reporting sexual violence victimization (Rape, Abuse & Incest National Network, 2019), the Catholic Priest scandal uncovered that fact between the years of 1950–2002, 81 percent of the children victimized by Catholic Priest were boys between the ages eleven tofourteen (John Jay College of Criminal Justice, 2004). Additionally, it was reported that the Boy Scout of America (BSA) sexual abuse scandal kept "perversion files that included over 12,200 young boys who alleged abuse by approximately 7,819 scout leaders throughout the country between the years of 1944–2016 (Christensen, 2019). According to Hetherington and Nunnally (2018), approximately 60 percent of sexually abused children experience abuse from trusted clergy and boy scout leaders and though abuse is widely known, proactive measures to protect children from sexual violence are not practiced and often ignored, thus supporting the denial and inaction from these youth social organizations. Moreover, these social institutions protect the perpetrator by maintaining and controlling the evidence which results in the information suppression of important documentation associated with DIIS Theory. In the case of the Boy Scouts of America, their "Ineligible Volunteer or Perversion" files contain the evidence that can be used against a perpetrator; however, with few convictions of sex offenders, families are forced to gather evidence to support their civil claims. To be clear, the normalization of sexual violence is masked in societal perceptions that often ignores and worse, fails to prosecute the victimization and vulnerability of youth. Nationally, 38% of child abuse is exposed and reported, thus resulting in the underreporting of sexual violent cases of minors and undetected sex abusers living in the community (Hetherington & Nunnally, 2018). Below is a narrative from David Pietrasanta who was repeatedly abused by his Boy Scout leader, Samuel L. Jones in California. His story is significant because he was one of the unreported Boy Scout cases that chose to speak out about the extensive abuse he experienced.

David and His Boy Scout Leader:
Fourteen years of Sexual Victimization

David was victimized by a regressed child sex abuser and did not tell anyone about the sexual violence until he became an adult. When David was eleven years old, his Boy Scout Leader asked his mother if he could give David tennis lessons. His mother gave her consent for the weekly lessons because she did not know that Scout Leader Jones was grooming her family to trust him while secretly engaging in violent sexual assaults of her son David after their weekly lessons. Samuel Leslie Jones would pick David up from the safety and comfort of his home and drive him to their tennis lesson. After the lesson, Samuel would take David to his apartment. It started as viewing pornographic videos and then he was invited into another room. David did not believe that he could escape or get the locks open on the front door, so he complied. Once in the room, Samuel placed his arm around him, and David felt pressure and restraint, "like being held in place." David was penetrated anally and aggressively. Jones's thrusts were quick and consistent. David was overpowered, fearful, and ashamed. Samuel was large in size, bigger, and much stronger than David. In order to avoid getting hurt, David believed that the best solution to prevent physical aggression was to comply with Samuel's request. "COMPLY" became the running thought loop that he repeated to himself during each sexual assault. It was his way of overcoming the frequent attacks. David experienced the first stage of denial. Samuel Jones's physically opposing structure caused David to feel powerless and deny his ability to control or prevent the sexual assault because he feared that he could overpower Samuel. David submits to Samuel's sexual aggression; his abuser is not concerned or sensitive to the pain and harm he caused David. Each encounter was filled with silence. Neither David nor Samuel spoke a word during the sexual violence. But David was small in size, and he did not believe that he had the power to stop Samuel. He recalls a picture of Jones as a scout leader standing behind a podium and the small size of his nine-year-old frame compared to Jones's massive size difference.

The second stage of inaction followed the initial rape. David did not tell his family that his scout leader abused him after his tennis lesson. According to David, Samuel was "so smooth and so slick" when dealing with David's family. It wasn't uncommon for David to come home and find Mr. Jones eating at his family's dinner table or visiting during the holidays. Mr. Jones served several roles in David's life; he was a scout leader, tennis coach, family friend and sexual predator. David later found out that Samuel adopted a son, Bobby, who lived in the home where the sexual attacks often occurred. Although David was concerned that Bobby would learn about the secret assaults, he did not tell anyone about the repeated sex abuse. Bobby would remain in his room with the door closed, during David's visits. David believed Samuel also abused Bobby. And Bobby would later commit suicide thus leading David to believe that Bobby's suicide was the result of years of sexual abuse. Furthermore, David's suppression of information (third stage of DIIS Theory) as a result of his feelings of powerlessness led him to conclude that he may have prevented the abuse if he took more steps to stop the years of abuse.

David's Regrets

Two of his most significant regrets are that he should have dated during his twenties and thirties and that he should have held his attacker accountable. He often looks at the huge settlements of money that people receive from their sexual assaults and his attacker was never held accountable. He referenced R. Kelly's payouts to his victims without conviction or sentencing. And it bugs him that he never received any money. Although, he does not believe that the money would have soothed him, he gets "ticked off" because David knows money would not help with the "inner stuff," but it would help with the "financial insecurity." David said that the statute of limitations expired and worked against him. He stated that the laws need to be changed, so that the statutes never run out. There was a time, at a very early age where he looked at every man as a child molester. Additionally, he believed that pedophiles of children follow similar addictive behaviors where addicts can "sniff" out other addicts.

Before David's therapist passed away, he, his mom, dad, two sisters, and brother arranged a family meeting. His brother was the first one he spoke about his years of sexual abuse and David's therapist believed it was best to get the family together for the Family Group on Saturdays to tell his family about the sexual assault from his troop leader. His mom took it the hardest because she believed that she did not "protect her kid." As the sexual abuse continued David sought drugs as a form of escape. His drug addiction increased as he got older. He was in rehab twenty-two times, arrested three times and homeless, sleeping in Encino Park, desperate to get off drugs. He reached out to his father for help. Filled with self-hatred, he never considered telling anyone that he was drowning in his own shame and guilt. His distorted idea of sex led to his earlier sexual experiences of excessive promiscuity, and a need to meet someone (all women) and have sex. David defined sex as having fun in the bars, clubs, and a lot of one-night stands. Falling in love was not part of the rules. Enjoying time with random women led to his current lifestyle—he never married because he believes he was emotionally unavailable.

In college, he dated one girl for eleven months. It was his belief that they broke up because of their religions. He was Catholic and she was Jewish, and he couldn't deal with the differences. He wasn't sure if he was in love, but he believed it was just fun having sex. The resentments that David continues to revisit and the various ways that his sexual maturity was stunted and deterred are associated with Samuel. Most people get married in their twenties and thirties or have a successful relationship. David was running away from "life and from himself," by using drugs. The long-term ramifications of trauma and arrested psychological development of sexual identity experienced by a sexually victimized person will be discussed in chapter five.

For twenty years, he looked at his rapes from every angle and the only factor he attributed to his healing was his sobriety and being able to live life "in reality." David managed to receive his college degree and while he did not believe that there was a structured career path for him, he became an addiction counselor working with the church and their program Vertiv: Saving God's Children. He currently raises awareness and educates adults on childhood sexual abuse. He found solace as a speaker for the church program, and it was this opportunity that was incredibly helpful for him. David wanted to protect his younger victimized self and felt bad that he did not protect that little boy. Attending AA meetings helps him recognize the progress of his healing. While he continues to relive the trauma of the abuse in his nightmares by occasionally waking up in a sweat, he must remind himself that it's 2019 and he is no longer Samuel's victim.

Like many victimized boys of child sex abuse cases, this extensive case of sexual abuse was not reported. While Samuel L. Jones was prosecuted in the 1980s for the sexual abuse of other boys during his service as a Boy Scout troop leader, he received probation and later moved from the community where the abuse occurred. The beloved Boys Scout of America (BSA) institution maintained and controlled the access to the Troop Leader files that would help families protect their children from predatory troop leaders. This act is associated with the DIIS theory of denial, inaction, and information suppression. BSA did not share the number of children victimized by their scout leaders and did not alert the families of the child abusers employed by them who were convicted and sentenced (Rowan, 2006). Since 2012, BSA was forced to release approximately 20,000 pages of documentation related to 1,200 child sex abuse cases (Dockterman, 2019). With over 12,000 children sexually abused between 1944–2016, by 7,800 scout leaders, the focal concerns theory was not implemented by law enforcement. Offender blameworthiness was associated with the stereotypes and intersection of gender, power, and status. Dockterman (2019) explains that children and families were intimidated by the assailants because they "often held influential positions in local churches, schools and businesses." The suppression of "P Files or Perversion Files" maintained by BSA contained information that did not keep the public safe (the second focal concern). David's abuser, Samuel Jones was sentenced to probation for the abuse of three boys. Additionally, it ignores the public and social cost of the prosecution and conviction of child sex abusers. It's difficult to believe that probation served as a deterrent for future abuse. More important, it did not address the psychological and emotional trauma that affected David's future intimate relationships and the two boys that were also victimized by Mr. Jones were not assessed for trauma.

In 1984, a family friend (lawyer) who lived with Samuel Jones reported that Mr. Jones had a family and lived in New Castle, Pennsylvania, and both were concerned that Jones had kids and would abuse them. Samuel's abuse stopped when David was twenty-five years old and he went to rehab. Traumatized, David was not able to look at pictures from the time he was abused by Samuel and cried when he thought about his helplessness. Although Jones was charged and received probation for the molestation of three boys from the California BSA troop, it did not give David solace and continues to affect his life today.

Incest & Examples of Regressed Sex Abusers

The second typology of sex offenders is associated with the regressed sex abuser. These offenders are often associated with intrafamilial sex abuse or incest and abusers that have sex with female adolescents (Simons, 2020). The regressed sex offender emerges in adulthood and is most likely associated with life stressors (i.e., unemployment, marital problems, financial setbacks, and threats to self-esteem and confidence (Robertiello & Terry, 2007). Their targets are often their own children or their children's friends because these groups are more readily accessible. However, a regressed offender will maintain adult sexual relationships and is not solely fixated on sexual relationships with children. Their sexual assault determinants are situational and associated with their poor coping skills as a result of their limited ability to address their loneliness, anxiety, and stress. According to the Office of Sex Offender Sentencing, Monitoring, Apprehending, Registering, and Trafficking (SMART) this group has lower recidivism rates (if given treatment) than other sex offender typologies (Simons, 2020). Yet, treatment is unlikely when sex offenders are undetected. Other researchers suggests that situational offenders may have experienced childhood sexual traumas (Horan & Beauregard, 2017). Regressed sex offenders with female victims report twice as many victims as their same-sex counterparts (Simons, 2020). Females are high risk victims for childhood sexual assault (Clayton, Jones, Brown, & Taylor, 2018). The next section of this chapter will use the oral narrative of Katalina (a pseudonym). Her sexual abuse history began at the age of five-years old. She recounts two cases of incest and molestation.

Katalina's Story of Incest—
My Grandfather & Uncle Molested Me

A proud forty-nine-year-old Dominican, Katalina's voice carries and her laugh is infectious as she recounts stories of incest. According to RAINN (2019), incest is unwanted sexual contact between family members. In

Katalina's case, she was sexually assaulted by her grandfather and uncle. This is a contradiction because in many Latin families, the men are staunch protectors of the women and girls and make every effort to keep them safe. However, with Katalina, the first assault happened when she was five years old at the hands of her grandfather, her mother's father. And although it only happened once, it has left an indelible mark upon her psyche. At the time of the assault, her grandfather had come for a visit and her mom was not at home. Needing groceries, her mom went out to pick up some items from the store and left her kids home with her father. Katalina's grandfather, seizing his opportunity, called Katalina into the room to watch TV with him. Immediately, when she sat on the bed, he laid her down making sure that she could still see the TV. When it appeared that Katalina was comfortable and engrossed in the TV program, her grandfather put his hands down her panties and penetrated her with his finger. While Katalina tells this part of the story with very little emotion, her lowered tone alerts me that this is something she may have wanted to keep secret. To date, she has never spoken to her mother about the sexual assault. Katalina's grandfather would be considered an intrafamilial child abuser (Seto, Babchishin, Pullman, & McPhail, 2015). However, Katalina's grandfather does not exhibit any of the anti-social tendencies often associated with pedophilia. They are more likely incest offenders that maintain adult relationships, possess limited psychopathic tendencies and report fewer male victims (Simons, 2020). According to Seto, Babchishin, Pullman & McPhail (2015), intrafamilial child abusers are more likely to have experienced some form of abuse (sexual, physical) and neglect in childhood and may score high on one or more traits of Finkelhor & Araji (1986) pedophilic four factor model (emotional congruence, child sexual arousal, blockage, and disinhibition). Past childhood trauma with arrested development and the use of symbols that help identify with their abuser can be attributed to emotional congruence. Additionally, sexual arousal to child pornographic images, and the psychological trauma associated with past abuse can also be associated with cultural blocks and inappropriate social skills and constraints that may have developed that allows the intrafamilial child abuser to ignore their sexual assaulting practices. Situational stressors with substance abuse and impulse disorder can contribute to incestuous responses.

My Uncle's Repeated Assaults

The second sexual assault was with her aunt's husband (her mother's aunt). Unlike the previous assault, these were a series of sexual assaults that spanned several years. The initial assault occurred when Katalina was nine years old. The family owned a flower shop and her aunt wanted Katalina to spend the night with her. As Katalina attempts to recall the initial assault, she believes her memory is inaccurate. She states that her uncle must have made earlier attempts to molest her because she was reluctant to sleep at her aunt's house for fear of her uncle sexualized behavior. She states that "there had to be other times" because she didn't want to go. But she remembers that she couldn't tell her mom that she didn't want to go because they would ask her why. The first, second, and third stages of DIIS theory are combined in Katalina's recall of past events because she experiences denial of her ability to control what her uncle did to her body. Next, she consents to the visit against her initial fears and exhibits inaction. Last, she engages in information suppression because she does not tell her mom about her uncle's behavior.

At that point she didn't know how to tell her mom what was happening. Emphatically, she explains that she "wasn't telling anyone what was happening." First, she was afraid, and it was her belief that her family would blame her for the abuse. More importantly, she was afraid that she would get in trouble or that her dad or favorite uncle (if they knew), would physically assault her aunt's husband. Her biggest fear was that her dad and uncle would get in trouble for protecting her and "they would be gone from her!" However, she experienced cognitive dissonance of conflicting conclusions—she did not want her family in jail for protecting her, but she believed that they weren't protecting her from her sexually abusive uncle.

At her aunt's apartment, Katalina played the entire time in the living room, and she stayed close to her aunt. She knew that if she remained in the room with her aunt, her uncle would not try anything. Strategizing to keep herself safe, her tactic worked because her uncle remained in the bedroom watching TV most of the day and evening. But once night fell, she began feeling nervous. She recalls thinking it was strange that her uncle had not come out of the room. Her aunt was sitting on the couch and Katalina moved back close to her aunt so she could sit next to her. But they both fell asleep. Katalina had fallen asleep on the floor, and she awoke with her uncle caressing her "whole ass." She stated that the fondling and molestation continued until about twelve to thirteen years old. As she got older, he got bolder and bolder. He was a forty-year-old man touching a pre-pubescent girl. Katalina's uncle sex offender typology can also be categorized as an intrafamilial sex abuser (Simons, 2020). He continued to maintain adult relationships such as the one he shared with Katalina's aunt and he did not possess the anti-social or psychopathic tendencies of substance usage and criminality (Seto, Babchishin, Pullman, & McPhail, 2015). However, life stresses may be associated with an apparent need to substitute a child for an adult sexual relationship. The incest taboo that admonishes sexual relationships with relatives may not be applicable because Katalina's uncle was not a genetic relative. In cases where there is declining sexual intimacy with the offender's partner and the child or teen serves in a surrogate maternal role (i.e., cleaning the house, taking care of younger siblings, running errands), she may be targeted by the abuser because of accessibility (Seto, Babchishin, Pullman, & McPhail, 2015; Simons, 2020). Katalina's aunt did not engage in sexual intercourse with Katalina's uncle. Furthermore, Katalina's uncle exhibits criteria of intrafamilial sex offenders such as (a) sexual entitlement and (b) offense supportive attitudes. Satisfaction of his sexual needs and teaching Katalina about the pleasures of sex was a desire her uncle expressed during various sexual violations. The sex offending behavior was misconstrued by her uncle to be beneficial to Katalina's sexual development.

Katalina adamantly believed that no one would learn what was happening to her when she visited her aunt's home or the flower shop. Yet when she eventually told her mom about the molestation after her uncle died, her mom was not shocked or surprised. Her mother explained that her uncle had tried to molest her and his "own daughter!" Astonished with this admission, it was then that Katalina immediately felt hatred for her mom because she could not believe that her mom had acknowledged that she was aware that her uncle molested little girls within the family but she allowed Katalina go to his home. Katalina believes her mom "fed her to the wolves" and she built up intense hatred for her because her mom failed to protect her. Over the years, her uncle "would grab her breasts, her ass, grope and feel her up" trying to take her pants off to touch her vagina. And she wouldn't let him, always pushing his hands away or pushing him off of her. But she remembers two occasions when he attempted to go further than just "groping" her.

She remembers one event when she was older, and she was riding in his car. He was always able to slide his hand in her underwear and massage her clitoris. She immediately realized he had established a boundary and did not seek penetration of her vagina. But there were a few times he got bold enough to attempt to penetrate her with his fingers and she would push him away. However, his most grievous attempt was when Katalina was asked to bring groceries to her aunt's house. When she got there, her aunt wasn't there but her uncle was waiting for her. It was then that Katalina knew her uncle would try to trap her in the house. She was unable to get away because she didn't have transportation back to her home.

She looked for her aunt and when she realized she wasn't there, her uncle trapped her in the room. She had entered the bedroom during her search, but when she turned around to leave, her uncle was behind her. He told her that her aunt had an errand to run but since she was gone, he said, "I just want to touch you!" Describing everything he wanted to do to her. He immediately pulled her pants down and this was the first time that he had ever been successful enough to get her pants down to her knees. He quickly pulled her panties down and asked, "has anyone ever done this to you" and he began performing oral sex on her. It was the first time that anyone had done this to her and Katalina was freaking out! Oddly, her freak out was because she was ashamed that "it felt good." She had never had this type of experience and secretly, she loved how it felt and he knew that she was responding to him. He continued the act for almost a minute and Katalina felt torn, and she pushed him away. He expressed that "she tasted so amazing!" Katalina flipped out and demanded that she be allowed to leave. Her uncle, knowing he had gone too far, complied and took her home. He wouldn't attempt to touch her again during the car ride. Katalina stated that every time she would use sternness, he would stop. She assumed that he went far enough but would not penetrate her so that he did not leave a trace of his sexual assaults.

To date, Katalina has told few people about her molestations. Only her brother (and I) know about her grandfather. Her mom, brother, two of her cousins, one of aunts and grandma know about her aunt's husband. Although she has never told her aunt about her husband, she has told his daughter and her children about the sexual assault. Katalina did not tell the family until she was in her late twenties. There was one reason for her revealing the truth about her uncle's behavior. With Katalina being raised alongside his grandkids, his daughter's kids believed him to be a hero. He was responsible for making the boys into men and although they loved Katalina like a sister, she believed that they had a warped idea about her uncle. They held him in high esteem.

They would often brag that he was "this great man, a great grandfather, a great husband, a great father, a great provider, a great role model but that's not her truth. Each time they made these statements in her presence, she would be filled with so much anger and fight back the need to scream out— "Oh my God, that's not even him." She would constantly fight back the urge not to blurt out the truth of her abuse, but one day she couldn't hold it back and in a car ride with her two cousins, her aunt, and her cousin's wife, she yelled out "well your superhero molested me when I was young!" The car went silent, and she immediately felt watery eyes, a knot in her throat and she believed at that that point she had been triggered so much that that's just how it came out. Katalina didn't want to tell them like that, but she told them that he had molested her for many years (ages nine and twelve). Her family was incredulous and appeared to be in total disbelief of her admission. One of her male cousins was like "what?" Sarcastically her response was like "how about that for a hero or role model?" She continued, it was almost like she was accusatory, "you guys had to know!" She crushed their image of him, and they resented her for it. She thinks that they didn't like how she brought it to light—so abruptly but at the time she just did not have any control over it. And she did not speak with them about the incident for a couple of months.

With her past experiences, Katalina is continues to be triggered by sexually aggressive men that are attracted to her—all of them! She has to force herself and put forth hand make huge effort to say no to them. The childhood sex abuse affected her ability to say no when she is in an intimate setting. Katalina feels as if she has to give in and she pushes herself to refocus and concentrate so that she doesn't feel as if she has to have sex with them. She equates these triggers to when she was younger, and she did not know how to say no and she did not have a chance to say no. When she finally began having sex, she states that she was extremely promiscuous and could not say no. The minute a guy would start touching her body or initiate sex, she was often scared to say no. While she did not think of her sexual assaults during these new encounters, she knew it prevented her from saying no. She recalls that she became empowered toward her uncle and the abuse stopped when she was twelve years old. However, he would sexually harass throughout the years. When she was sixteen years of age, she became pregnant and she found herself alone with her uncle in the flower shop. He walked up behind and whispered to her—"You should have told me you were having sex!" A confused Katalina turned around and asked him "Why?" She was so confused. Her uncle exclaimed, "he would have loved to have tasted that first!" It was then that she felt disgust. She explains that this was the first time she felt disgust and believes that it was due to the fact that she was sexually active with boys her age. Katalina believes that much of the sexually abusive events have been repressed and there is a blockage. She believes that her history may best explain her sexual orientation. Katalina identifies as bisexual. Ninety percent of her experiences have been with men, but she remembers that she has always been attracted to and experimented with girl cousins and friends. She has initiated several sexual encounters with other girls. Yet she is not sure if the molestation by her grandfather may have pushed her to engage in bisexual experiences.

Katalina often feels unworthy of love, and these thoughts bring her to tears.

She explains that she can talk about the sexual assaults a million times and she is fine, but when she thinks about all the issues that she has with herself, she wonders if she would have ever felt that way if she had not been sexually assaulted repeatedly. It's her belief that the sexual assaults created low self-esteem, and she will never feel worthy because of it. When she looks at herself in the mirror and recalls her struggles with body issues, and her limited self-worth, she is unable to see herself as "someone to be loved." Although many of her friends have told her, I wish you could see yourself as we see you, she does not believe she ever will see herself the way they see her. Katalina believes that she has yet to be with someone who really loved her or respected her completely. More importantly, she does not know if she could receive love from those that want to shower her with both love and respect.

The next section will investigate Chicago Public School's (CPS) application of DIIS theory, and the institutional negligence exhibited in numerous schools after approximately six hundred complaints of sex abuse in their school district were reported to administrators (i.e., principals and teachers) and the CPS Office of the Inspector General (Leone & Jackson, 2019). Many of the complaints included groping and penetration from juvenile offenders. The focus of this section will examine juvenile offenders and highlight their differences from adult offenders.

Title IX Failures in Chicago Public Schools (Grades K-12)

In the third largest public school district, amidst the height of the #MeToo movement, girls in grades K-12 were victimized in the Chicago Public School (CPS) system and their complaints were repeatedly ignored (Jackson, Smith Richards, Marx, & Perez Jr., 2018). Over six hundred cases of sexual violence were identified by a U.S. Department of Education Office for Civil Rights (OCR) investigation conducted between 2015 and 2016 based on two reported complaints against the district of sexual assault (Green, 2019). However, the OCR investigation found "2,800 cases of sexual violence between students and 280 cases between adult and students that dated back to 2012" (Leone & Jackson, 2019). Kenneth Marcus, the assistant secretary for OCR explained that although the #MeToo movement focused on sexual violence on college campuses, there were widespread problems at the "elementary and secondary school." (Modan, 2019). One of the reasons for the mishandling of hundreds of sexual assault cases is that Chicago Public School neglected to hire a Title IX district coordinator from 1999-2016. When an interim coordinator was finally hired in 2019, his powers and authority were limited in scope. Staff members that were responsible for handling complaints did not follow the federal guidelines imposed by Title IX and often did not report the sexual abuses to law enforcement agencies (Jackson, Smith Richards, Marx, & Perez Jr., 2018). Chicago state laws mandate all school staff and officials to report sexual assaults on their campuses to law enforcement and child welfare services. The DIIS theory of the denial of the offender as a threat, the inaction of school staff and administrators to report the incidents to law enforcement and information suppression of the offender's acts in order to assign accountability and keep other students safe are examples of repeated negligence. An investigation of the "egregious" malfeasance of school officials' failure to take action when sex crimes were repeatedly reported or the use of relaxed background checks and hiring practices of sex offenders led victims to report the allegations to the Chicago Tribune.

Reporters studied ten years (2008–2017) of police data in order to identify the number of sexual assaults cases that took place because CPS refused to provide the requested data. This behavior is associated with the third stage of DIIS theory, information suppression. After the threat of litigation, CPS yielded and submitted the statistics. Findings showed that sexual crimes against students by adult staff average three per day in a district with approximately 355,000 students (Leone, Hundreds of new sex abuse or misconduct allegations involving CPS students reported since September. "What can we do to prevent this?," 2019). In one case, a student athlete reported that she was raped by her coach, Gerald Gaddy over forty times in his office (Jackson, Smith Richards, Marx, & Perez Jr., 2018). Yet another coach, Dino Amendola, with a previous felony conviction would later be fired for "having sex with an eighteen-year-old student." But Illinois age of consent laws permit sex between students and adults once the student reaches his/her seventeenth birthday (Jackson, Marx, Perez Jr., & Smith Richards, 2018). Amendola impregnated the student that believed she was in love with the coach. A student that was gang raped in a classroom was asked to transfer to another school by a staff member who believed the move of the victim would be easier than moving the predators of the sexual assault. A tenured teacher with a twenty-year history of sexually inappropriate touch, lewd comments, and groping was reported to child welfare agencies but was reinstated "several weeks later" by the principal and asked to take a workshop on sexual misconduct (Green, 2019). The reinstatement of the sex offender by the principal can be attributed to the first stage of denial because the administrator may not believe the teacher a threat to the children and teens that attend the school. Race, ethnicity, socioeconomic status did play a role in the number sexual assault and rape cases identified by the Chicago Tribune and the OCR investigations. Preparatory schools, magnate schools, and schools within impoverished neighborhoods were all targets for sexual predation (Jackson, Smith Richards, Marx, & Perez Jr., 2018). The current chief executive officer, Janice Jackson, was sickened that students were "harmed" and overwhelmed by the number of cases identified in her school district (Schulte, 2018). She vowed to train all staff on mandatory reporting guidelines from the "top" level officials to the "bottom." In 2018, the Department of Education withheld $4 million dollars of federal funding as a result of the improper handling of sex assault cases. More important, they would demand oversight of future cases and the placement of a "Title IX team in order to address the systemic problem areas (Green, 2019). But the Department of Education is also negligent due to their lack of oversight of the Chicago Public School and the need for a Title IX district coordinator that reviewed the sexual assault cases and provided annual reporting. The data of the systemic problem spanned approximately ten years (2008–2018) but DOE did not intervene until complaints surfaced in media reports (Leone & Jackson, 2019). However, their investigation came too late because the damage had been done; victims no longer trusted their teachers, officials, or law enforcement to help them after sexual assault claims were launched. Many were subjected to repeated interrogations, ridiculed by other students, and bullied when favored but suspected predatory teachers went to jail (Jackson, Smith Richards, Marx, & Perez Jr., 2018). More important, victims often remained in classes with juvenile offenders. The negative responses of observing students after victims' reporting can be aligned with the blaming and shaming of victims by peers, and societal members (Ramirez, Jeglic, & Calkins, 2015). The negligence of the Chicago Public School system shows that in spite of the #MeToo movement, administrative changes and policy can be a slow process.

Juvenile Sex Offenders

According to the Office of Sex Offender Sentencing, Monitoring, Apprehending, Registering, and Tracking (2020), approximately 25 percent of sex offenders are juveniles and are responsible for 40 percent of the sexual assaults committed in the United States (Przybylski & Lobanov-Rostovsky, 2020). Due to their age (minors under age eighteen), juvenile sex offenders (JSO) are treated significantly differently than their adult counterparts. The methods used by the states for JSO is the attribution of accountability and rehabilitation (McCuish & Lussier, 2017) while adult sex offenders are given the option of treatment intervention (i.e., cognitive behavioral, group therapy, etc.) in order to reduce re-offending (Marques, Wiederanders, Day,

Nelson, & van Ommeren, 2005). Various forms of rehabilitation programs are provided to JSO in order to combat recidivism and the reduction of the potential for lifelong sex offending. However, when explaining the differences between adult sex offenders and JSO, the age of the juvenile, the psychosexual and cognitive development, and past sexual victimization must be considered in order to provide appropriate diagnosis, treatment, and length of rehabilitation (Leversee, 2017).

The etiology associated with juvenile sexual offenders falls into different categories (Johnson, 2018). Past sexual victimization of juvenile sex offenders, types of sexual behavior used during victimization, relationship of perpetrator to victim, personality traits of the juvenile sex offender, and type of home environment of the perpetrator (Leversee, 2017). JSO were once victims and often engage in sexual play behaviors that mimic their sexual victimization experiences with other children and peers (Johnson, 2018; Leversee, 2017). For juveniles that were sexually assaulted at young ages (three to seven years old) and for long periods of time, the effects of sexual victimization were much more severe and detrimental to their psychological, cognitive and sexual development (Leversee, 2017). In a study of sixty-one female juvenile sex offenders and 122 juvenile male sex offenders living in Texas, the researchers compared the sexual victimization behaviors utilized by both groups. (Vandiver & Teske, 2006).

Using randomization, one female JSO was matched with two male JSO on age and race. Findings showed that the average age of victims for both male and female JSO was under the age of nine. Female JSO victims were approximately seven and sixty-hundredths years old and the average age of male JSO victims was eight and forty-hundredths years old. Males were more likely to victimize girls (approximately 70 percent) and females were likely to victimize both males (41 percent) and females (59 percent). Both male and female JSO engaged in intrafamilial victimization. It is important to note that all JSO in this study were sexually victimized as children and some were both physically and sexually abused and this factor is associated with intrafamilial sex offenses (Vandiver & Teske, 2006; Leversee, 2017; Johnson, 2018). Therefore, abusive home environment must be considered when investigating juvenile sex offenders. Furthermore, female JSO are more likely to sexually assault victims under twelve years old when engaging in babysitting or caregiving situations that included relatives or acquaintances (Vandiver & Teske, 2006). The personality traits of the JSO was also examined and can be a factor that attributes to sex offenses.

Characteristics of juvenile sex offenders can be categorized as sexual aggression, antisocial pathology, sexual: impulsivity, fantasy, and inadequacy

(Leversee, 2017). In a study that investigated ninety-three male juvenile offenders, personality traits of juvenile sex offenders, juvenile non sex offenders, and the control group were assessed (Margari, et al., 2015). Researchers found that JSOs were more likely to exhibit avoidance distraction coping tendencies, were more prone to lie, showed limitations in academic performance, and identified earlier sexual experiences than their non sex offenders and the control group. Moreover, in a study that consisted of 351 adolescent male juvenile sexual offenders that were adjudicated for sexual crimes against children, peers, and adults, researchers confirmed the previous character traits (Joyal, Carpentier, & Martin, 2016). Findings showed that JSOs were physically and sexually abused (approximately 66 percent), 54 percent were socially isolated or were rejected by peer groups, 58 percent possessed sexual deviant fantasies. Additionally, JSOs were more likely to be diagnosed with conduct disorder, ADHD, and the use psychostimulant medications. They also exhibited aggressive and interpersonal violence. The legal ramifications associated with juvenile sex offenders are also different from adult sex offenders and may include the following (McCuish & Lussier; Fox & DeLisi, 2018):

a. JSO detected by law enforcement but evidence did not support the charge and sanctions are not imposed on the youth.
b. JSO are given the opportunity to provide a guilty plea for lesser crime after sex offense charge (i.e., assault)
c. Charged by the court but JSO is not guilty of the sex offense
d. Found guilty of serious sex crime such as sexual homicide.

Furthermore, the age of the victim(s), if consent was provided, and the cognitive development of the victim is considered. When victims are minors (under the age of thirteen), they are not able to provide consent because of their cognitive ability to comprehend the nature of the sexual act. For example, children that are five years old are not able to provide consent or provide cogent descriptions of the sexual assault when questioned by law enforcement. Other examples with complex legal consequences to consider is when the JSO and the victim are (peers) or the victim is a minor and the offender is an adolescent and consent may be provided but concludes with aggression and/or violence (McCuish & Lussier, 2017). Still, there are JSO that are undetected by law enforcement because the sexual assault was not reported. Studies have shown that JSO may be influenced by peers, have limited self-regulation, management skills, and finite judgment competencies (Ueda, 2017; McCuish & Lussier, 2017; Przybylski & Lobanov-Rostovsky, 2020). When defining JSO typologies, Ueda (2017) extends the criteria to include a criminal history, impulsivity, empathy, depression, psychosis, and childhood sexual abuse. Przybylski & Lobanov-Rostovsky (2020) emphasize risk taking and reckless behavior must also be associated with the juvenile sex offender.

Kyle's Story of Incest—My cousin molested me

Kyle, a thirty-something highly educated millennial was insistent that a male perspective that experienced sexual assault be included in this book. Unlike some males, Kyle did not remain silent about his early childhood sexual abuse. There are few people that know about his assault, his grandmother, one of his younger sisters, his wife, and me. Like many rapes and sexual assaults, Kyle's assault began in a place that he considered safe, his grandmother's house. As a young boy, he lived there with his mother, three sisters, and an uncle. At five years old, an older cousin named Nicole (Nikki), related through marriage, came to live with him and his family. She was approximately six to seven years older than he and came from a troubled background. Her mother was strung out on drugs with thirteen kids and his grandmother took Nikki in to give her a home. Kyle's mom was not happy with his grandmother's decision to bring her cousin into the house and wanted his grandmother to focus only on her grandchildren. Kyle remembers Nikki living in his home for approximately one to two years before she began running away. His grandmother would allow Nikki to babysit him when she needed to step out of the house for a few minutes or an hour. He recalls it was this "alone time" that gave Nikki the opportunity to create the conditions she needed to fondle and molest Kyle.

Sexual Assault

Nikki would tell Kyle, "let's play" and they would play house. He never felt afraid of her. She would touch his genitals and wanted him to touch her "private parts." Very often, Nikki wanted both of them naked and would get the covers and they would grope each other for approximately a half hour to one hour. Although he does not believe she reached orgasm, he liked the touching and would become aroused by her touch. Playing house did not simply consist of naked foreplay but when they were finished they would begin normal play behavior. None of the adults in the house suspected that Kyle or Nikki were engaging in sex play and his grandmother typically returned home within the hour. Kyle was excited to play with Nikki because she often gave him praise and positive reinforcement to encourage his continued "touching and feeling" of each other. She would tell him, "you're good at this." He did not feel any remnants of guilt or shame surrounding these sexual assaults. As a result of the molestation, Kyle began to act out, thus touching little girls his age as his cousin had touched him. As previously purported, female juvenile sex offenders are more likely to target younger children (in this case a relative), that they are babysitting and are relatives (Vandiver & Teske, 2006; Leversee, 2017; Johnson, 2018). As the victim, Kyle was rewarded with praise from Nikki and later introduced the sexual behaviors that he learned to vulnerable and naïve peers.

Accusations of Sex Play with Other Kids

There were several occurrences when Kyle would touch girls his age inappropriately and their mothers would tell his mother and grandmother about the behaviors he engaged in with their daughters. He explained that, at the time, nothing was done about his inappropriate touching because no one believed that he would engage in those "types of behaviors." The adults in Kyle's life engaged in denial, inaction, and information suppression (DIIS theory). Future visits with other children were permitted and unsupervised. Moreover, the nature of his sexual play behavior was not discussed with the other parents. He further explains that there were two times when these accusations came up surrounding his inappropriate touch of other little girls his age. Once, when his mom's friend and her daughters would come to the house and another time was at a babysitter's home with another young girl. And although, Kyle would later tell his grandmother about his repeated sexual assaults by his cousin, his grandmother immediately recalled a time when Kyle was at her girlfriend's home, and he was accused of touching another little girl there. Two steps of DIIS theory can be associated with his grandmother's response to keep his secret. First, her behavior can be attributed to inaction and information suppression. His grandmother did not alert Kyle that she was aware of his behavior in the earlier stages of his development when she learned of his sex play with little girls from her girlfriend. Next, she did not alert Kyle's mother about the allegations and did not divulge his secret when Kyle recounts other incidences of sexual misconduct. Moreover, Kyle and his grandmother believed that Nikki targeted and touched Kyle to "spite" and seek revenge against his mother's reaction to Nikki living in the home. As a child, Kyle's did not believe there was something wrong when he played with Nikki. He believed that this was typical play behavior of children, and this was the type of play he engaged in with girls his age. After the accusations, he learned that it was not "okay" to touch people in their genital area, and he was never accused again of inappropriate touch. As he got older, he simply sought girls that were okay with him touching them in their "private parts" and he admits that he became sexually active at fourteen years old, an earlier age than other teens that he knew.

Hypersexual Activities

He explained that he could identify these girls by their upbringing, typically those that his family knew very well that were periodically brought to his home where both families could get together to play cards or other events. With parents in one room and kids playing in another room, they would engage in sex play without their parent's knowledge. There was "no penetration," but naked fondling and touching each other. He believes that the earlier molestation resulted in his openness to other, more specifically, bisexual experiences.

While he was receptive to and would allow willing males to give him hand jobs and oral sex (twice), he would not reciprocate because he believed he was, and is, not attracted to males. He admits that oral sex with boys "just wasn't the same as it was with girls." Additionally, he states that he has always had multiple sex partners and he attributes this to the earlier sexual assault. He considers his sexual appetite to be heightened and rates it at an eight (scale of one [low] to ten [high]). Throughout his teenage years and high school, he sought girls that were willing partners. These girls were those he either knew through sports or family friendships and he did not consider himself to be a predator towards unassuming girls that consented to these sexual encounters.

He admits that he never became a predator or considered fondling younger girls because he had sisters, had helped raise them, and changed their diapers. He was hyper vigilant towards people when his sisters around other men in the family. But he does recall a series of sex play activities with a cousin (girl) who was six months younger than he and these experiences would last for three years (between nine to twelve years old). He defined these activities as exploratory but also the re-creation of the behaviors he learned with Nikki.

Sensory Triggers and Sex

Kyle recalls a specific beauty supply lotion (coconut and other flavors) as a sensory trigger. Nikki would use the lotion on his penis and he would rub it on her body. While he no longer sees Nikki (it's been over twenty years), he does continue to see the other cousin who engaged in sex play with him during the ages of nine and twelve years. His does not believe that the earlier sexual assaults resulted in the creation of fetishes, but he confesses that he has engaged in orgies with three and four women and uses porn to hold him over until the next sexual encounter. He has admitted to daily porn viewing and uses it as a substitute for sex, but he would not call it an addiction. He states that he simply views porn when he is not engaging in sexual intercourse frequently. If he has sex regularly, he can "go for months" without watching porn, but his wife is not aware that Kyle watches porn. And his selection of porn is not related to his earlier sexual experiences with Nikki. He did not identify any porn preferences.

The Importance of Telling "His" Story

Kyle's early introduction to sex play has significantly influenced his sexual experiences, yet he was adamant that his story needed to be told. He says there are male family members and friends that he knows who have been sexually abused or raped during early developmental stages and the numbers (statistics) are real. He expressed that "it [sexual assault] happens" and he had recently felt that he had hit a point where he was at rock bottom. A faculty member told him to seek help from a therapist and it weighed on his mind to talk to someone. He wanted to find someone he could trust to tell the story of his past experiences in order to regain some stability. It was, and is, his belief that stories about how males are affected by sexual assault should be part of the narrative.

Summary

In conclusion, this chapter explored various forms of sex offenders that abuse children and teens. Each typology and the characteristics associated with their behaviors is detailed in order to investigate the psychological and cognitive motivations associated with sex offenders. Additionally, juvenile sex offenders' typologies were also introduced in order to examine the repercussions of sexual victimization of youth. Three oral narratives provided raw data that explained the "lived" experiences of children's vulnerability to adult and juvenile sex offenders. The application of DIIS Theory was applied to each narrative in order provide additional definitions of the ways denial, inaction, and information suppression can affect different groups of people at various stages of sexual abuse. Chapter 4 will explore teens' and adults' psychological and cognitive experiences of sexual assaults.

CHAPTER FOUR

~

Teen and Adult Sexual Assault

Teens, sexual violence, and victimization statistics are increasing and well documented Finkelhor, 1994; Goldbaum, et al. 2003; Finkelhor, Ormrod, & Turner, 2007). Decades of research has revealed the growing number of adolescents who are vulnerable and potential victims of sexual assault are also more likely to be re-victimized in (Classen, et al. 2005; Finkelhor, Ormrod, & Turner, 2007; Papalia, et al, 2017). Most of the research regarding teens and sexual violence often includes statistics associated with children (under age ten). Additionally, it combines data associated with sexual abuse and sexual assault (Moles and Leventhal 2014). According to Finkelhor, Shattuck, et al. (2014), sexual abuse is defined as intrafamilial sexual victimization from a family member (parent, older sibling, etc.) or an extrafamilial adult serving in a caregiver role (coach, teacher, babysitter, etc.) and the youth had frequent or recurring interactions. Sexual assault was described as sexual victimization from strangers or same-age peers (Moles and Leventhal, 2014). According to the National Sexual Violence Resource Center (2018), one in three rape victims were between the ages of eleven and seventeen years old and most reported that they knew the offender. With the sexual violence of teens and young adults steadily increasing (Finkelhor, Shattuck, et al., 2014; Moles & Leventhal, 2014, Papalia, 2017), prevention should help this vulnerable population learn how to protect themselves from acquaintances and family members. The goal of this chapter is to identify the issues that youth (pre and post-pubescent) face as victims of sexual assault. Empirical studies, cases from the media, and oral narratives will be included in order to examine the sexual victimization of minors and the DIIS Theory of denial, inaction and information suppression. DIIS theory will be applied to these cases in order to establish institutional and familial neglect of victim's needs.

Sexual Victimization of Teens & Young Adults

Adolescence is a time when youth are at high risk of sexual victimization as an outcome of sexual exploration (Finkelhor, Shattuck, et al. 2014; Campbell, et al. 2015; Banvard-Fox, et al. 2020). Some victimized teens that have experienced more than one sexual assault, report that they were first assaulted in their teens (Basile, Chen and Saltzman 2007). Moreover, these youths are less likely to seek medical attention or report their sexual victimization and it is this reason that national statistics are often inaccurate because of the large number of underreported cases (Finkelhor, Shattuck, et al. 2014; Campbell, et al. 2015). With adolescent males, their assaults may occur during organized sports (Hartill 2009). Using a pooled sample of 2,293 teens between the ages of fifteen and seventeen, Finkelhor, Shattuck et al (2014) found that most of the reported sex assaults were committed by juvenile offenders for both males and females. The reported cases of sexual assault were offenders that the victims knew. Moreover, as victims aged, the prevalence of sexual assault increased. With fifteen-year-old, 16.8 percent of females and 4.3 percent of males reported sexual assault or abuse, but with seventeen-year-olds, 26.6 percent of females and 5.1 percent of males reported sexual assault or abuse. However, with both males and females, penetration was the least likely to be reported in the youth sample. Other studies have linked the increasing frequency of sexual victimization with other forms of abuse (physical, emotional, neglect, etc.), sexual bullying. These issues are known as polyvictimization (Finkelhor, Ormrod, & Turner, 2007; Pittenger, Huit and Hansen, 2016) and for youth with a history of childhood sexual assault, re-victimization in older adolescence and young adulthood is projected (Classen, Palesh, and Aggarwal, 2005; Pittenger, Huit, and Hansen, 2016). Once a teen is sexually assaulted, their chances of re-victimization increase in adulthood (Papalia, et al. 2017).

Factors the May Predict Sexual Re-Victimization

In home environments where abuse and violence is normalized, sexual assault and abuse is present (Walsh et al., 2013; Ullman, 2016; Ullman and Relyea, 2016; Papalia, Mann and Ogloff, 2020). Youth that experienced past sexual abuse or assault possess low sexual control and may engage in sexual risk taking behaviors (i.e., substance usage, multiple sex partners) (Walsh et al., 2013). Additionally, psychological stressors that may be remnants of previous sexual assault or interpersonal violence including emotional dysregulation, self-blame, denial, PTSD symptoms, and emotional difficulties may be contributing factors to revictimization (Papalia, Mann and Ogloff, 2020). Limitations in sexual refusal assertiveness may prevent youth from declining unsolicited sexual advances (Basile, Chen & Salzman, 2007; Relyea & Ullman, 2016; Banvard-Fox et al., 2020; Papalia, Mann and Ogloff, 2020). In a three year longitudinal study conducted in Chicago, 1,863 females participants were assessed each year (with each year identified as a wave for a total of three waves) (Ullman and Relyea, 2016). Approximately 60.7 percent of the women reported a history of childhood sexual abuse in wave one, lived in negative social environments, and possessed maladaptive coping skills with psychological stressors associated with denial, self-blame, and emotional numbness. In wave two and three, fourty-nine reported re-victimization with higher rates found in wave two (one year after the wave one reporting). These findings were consistent with a study previously conducted by Walsh et al., 2013 with 546 college aged females reporting either a substance related rape (52 percent) and a forcible rape (27 percent) since the age fourteen. Low perceived control was negatively correlated with re-victimization, child sexual abuse, and the ability to determine the cues associated with sexual and alcohol related experiences. Furthermore, the solutions adopted by K-12 school administrators and institutions can include denial of the facts, inaction in reporting, information suppression combined with the blaming and shaming of victims that can contribute to their powerlessness.

Denial, Inaction, Information Suppression (DIIS) with Teens and Young Adults

In K-12 schools across America, sexual assault is becoming more pervasive (Kitchener 2019). But the school responses for the youth that file sexual assault complaints are to blame and shame the victim with suspension or expulsion for the violation of the school's sexual conduct code. Strict sexual conduct codes such as indecent exposure and sexual impropriety are used as retaliatory methods against teens that file sexual assault complaints. For example, the Fayetteville Board of Education neglected to investigate the sexual assault of sixteen-year-old girl identified as A. P. when she was grabbed repeatedly by her neck, sexually assaulted, and forced to perform oral sex on a boy in her class (McLaughlin 2019). Moreover, she was punished as a result of her sexual victimization, her phone was confiscated, she was given a ten-day in-school suspension and after an investigation, expelled for the rest of the school year (National Women's Law Center 2019). This is not uncommon in schools that enforce zero tolerance policies with punitive consequences. The Fayetteville Board of Education's decision to expel the victim and label her abuse as an act of sexual impropriety is a violation of the Title IX sex discrimination. Title IX guidelines include incidences of sexual harassment, assault, and rape under sex discrimination violations (U.S. Department of Health & Human Services, 2021). All schools: primary, secondary universities and colleges that receive any form of federal funding, including financial aid resources are expected to create and encourage an environment that is free of sex discrimination and sexual violence (RAINN, 2021). This is also associated with the focal concerns theory of offender blameworthiness, maintenance of public safety, and the costs of societal consequences: punishment and prosecution (Campbell & Fehler-Cabral, 2018). Once an administrator is made aware of a report of sexual harassment, assault, or rape, the school must take immediate steps to investigate and address the sexually violent incident. The Title IX coordinator must be contacted, and the victim and offender must be informed of their Title IX rights in order to maintain compliance. But in the previously mentioned case, the school administrator believed that incident was consensual and did not consider the Title IX procedures thus applying DIIS theory to the process of investigation.

When K-12 institutions and their administrators neglect to comply with Title IX regulations without enforcement of an environment free of sexual discrimination, they deny a victim of their civil rights and a thorough investigation. This is considered part of the denial, inaction, and information Suppression or DIIS theory. Additionally, the school administrator in the above-mentioned case failed to contact the Title IX coordinator which is considered inaction. Each school district is assigned at least one Title IX coordinator and that person must be contacted when acts of sexual violence are committed in the district. Information suppression occurred when the administrator neglected to alert the victim of her Title IX rights or provide contact information for the Title IX coordinator. Cases of Title IX non-compliance associated with denial, inaction, and information suppression (DIIS) in K-12 schools and neighborhoods across America have become more problematic.

Title IX Failures in K-12

In an Oregon school district, Emily, a sixteen-year-old sexual assault survivor was assaulted by a male classmate while "high" (Kingkade, 2017). In October 2015, Emily reported the incident to two school administrators but by December 2016, she and her mom were not informed of the outcome of the investigation. She was never instructed of her Title IX rights, nor was she given the contact information of the Title IX coordinator for her school district. Emily left the school for medical reasons and received her GED online, but a Facebook post from her attacker prompted her to alert the public of her sexual assault. Her attacker had identified the methods he used to sexually assault teenage girls under the influence of a substance. Furthermore, he mentioned Emily by name in his post because she had reported him to the police. The Ashland school officials that were initially alerted of the sexual assault engaged in denial, inaction, and information suppression or DIIS theory and failed to comply with Title IX procedures. Like the previous case, they denied Emily the right to a comprehensive investigation, failed to contact the Title IX coordinator, a form of inaction and did not offer a printed list of her Title IX rights nor provide the contact information of the coordinator to Emily or her mother (information suppression). When institutions fail to act in sexual assault cases, undetected assailants continue to victimize unsuspecting teens. When Emily responded to her abuser's Facebook post, she explained the details of the assault and added that the school did not investigate the issue. Once Emily's post was shared, another victim came forward. However, the school was negligent in their role to comply with Title IX guidelines of an environment free of sex discrimination that includes sexual harassment, assault, and violence (U.S. Department of Health & Human Services, 2021). Ironically, teens like Emily and another victim of sexual assault from Ashland High School named Bella have begun to fight back when schools failed to protect them. Although a school investigation was conducted and measures employed to prevent Bella's assailant from coming to campus when Bella was attending, Ashland school administrators neglected to enforce the sanctions. Her assailant continued to visit the campus when Bella was in attendance. Bella, along with other outraged students, staged a sit-in, printed "Got Consent" t-shirts and wrist bands, and created a Survivor's Circle as a result of school administrators' inability to address accountability measures for sexual assault offenders. Her activism would later change the ways Ashland school district complied with Title IX sex discrimination (Kingkade, 2017). School administrator negligence can be found in other states across America.

In the Redland Unified School District in California, approximately twenty teachers and school administrators were accused of sexual misconduct, inappropriate sexual behavior, and assault over a ten year period (Van Zandt 2021). Although many of the administrators were aware of the assaults, they failed to report it to the Title IX district coordinator or law enforcement.

These negligent actions can further be associated with DIIS theory of denial, inaction, and information suppression. From 1999–2001, Sean Ramiro Lopez, an eighth grade English teacher molested four boys that he invited to his home for "growth enhancing hormone" treatment (Mensching 2006). Lopez measured the youths' penis before and after erection and requested that the boys masturbate while watching pornographic videos. Additionally, each male was given growth pills as part of the treatment and once erect, Lopez removed semen from the youth's body with a syringe. Reports indicate that students alerted Marilyn Kemple, the principal of Clement Middle School that Lopez would bring pictures of naked women to show to twelve- to thirteen-year-old boys, but she did not investigate the sexual misconduct or alert law enforcement (Van Zandt 2021). Kemple would later retire in 2004 but her actions can easily be applied to denial, inaction, and information suppression when she neglected to adhere to Title IX regulations which required the promotion of a school environment free of sex discrimination. Moreover, she did not alert the Title IX coordinator or law enforcement (denial), warn the survivors of their Title IX rights, or provide contact information (inaction and information suppression). Lopez continued to teach until 2005 but was sentenced to seventy-four years in prison in 2006. During the trial, the defense attorneys used the victim blaming defense stating that the males "failed to exercise reasonable effort to protect themselves" from the sexual assault perpetrated by Lopez (Mensching 2006). Victim blaming tactics used by defense attorneys are not uncommon in sexual assault cases throughout the country (Yarbough 2021). They imply that the victims have some modicum of control during a sex crime. When the offender is an authority figure, powerful, or dominant adult, and the victim is young, naïve, and vulnerable, intersectionality must be applied and considered.

New allegations were against Lopez were reported in 2020 when seven of Lopez's former students (now in their thirties) sued the Redland Unified School District administrators' and Lopez for the sexual abuse they suffered. Focal concerns theory can be applied to this case that includes (a) offender blameworthiness, (b) desire to protect the community from threat, and (c) imposition of constraints and consequences that result in few convictions and the blaming and shaming of victims. When considering the actions of the principal Kemple, she failed to recognize the power of Lopez's authority, ability to manipulate, and abuse the trust the youth showed toward him. Moreover, she did not hold Lopez accountable for his sexual misconduct by launching an investigation in order to keep the rest of the school community safe from future sexual assaults that may be committed by Lopez. Last, she did not restrict Lopez's sexual misconduct or impose consequences that limited his interactions with vulnerable students. Title IX violations in K-12 schools mimic the issues that young adults face in college, university and work settings. The next section will explore the sexual assaults of young adults and the use of non-disclosure agreements (NDAs).

Sexual Assault: College Students & Young Adults

If you are a young adult and attending college, you are in the highest risk category for sexual assault (The Association of American Universities [AAU], 2019). Moreover, if you are female, a college student and between the ages of eighteen to twenty-four, you are three times more likely to experience sexual assault than young males while non-college students are four times more likely to be a victim of sexual violence or misconduct (Rape, Abuse, Incest National Network [RAINN] 2020). In a 2019 Campus Climate Study on Sexual Assault and Misconduct, 181,752 college students attending thirty-three college and universities (public/private) completed the self-report survey. To date, it is the largest probability sample that explores the sexual victimization and issues in this high-risk population. Furthermore, there was an increase in nonconsensual sexual contact previous surveys conducted by AAU in 2015 and 2017 reported by women (26 percent), men (7 percent), transgender/genderqueer/nonbinary (TGQN) (23 percent) in which physical force was used (Smith-Kimble 2021). One of the most prevailing issues found in the 2019 study is the underreporting of sexual assault and rape cases. The relationship between victim and offender can be attributed to the underreported statistics (AAU, 2019; Smith-Kimble, 2021). Approximately 80 percent of the victims know the perpetrator (i.e., intimate partner, friend, date, acquaintance) and were attacked near or in their homes (AAU, 2019). Substance usage is often reported with nonconsensual sexual victimization and the relationship between the victim and perpetrator can be attributed to underreporting (Richards 2016). Many did not wish to alert law enforcement or campus administrators because of self-blame, substance usage, fear of retaliation, or did not want to accuse the offender (Richards, 2016; AAU, 2019; RAINN; 2021; Smith-Kimble, 2021). Others have not utilized campus resources and support (i.e., counseling) because of acceptability of the consequences associated with the previously mentioned issues regarding underreporting and help seeking (Holland and Cortina 2017). For some, the outcome of Title IX investigations, hearings, and use of non-disclosure agreements may serve as barriers that promote awareness and aid prevention. The Clery Act requires that colleges and universities that receive Title IX funding must publish crime statistics for the public related to sexual assault and rape, alert the campus of the sexual assault (identities remain anonymous) in a timely manner and provide the victim and offender with the outcome of the investigation (U.S. Department of Justice 2014). Outcomes of campus investigations may deter students from reporting and impose the use of non-disclosure agreements (Limining 2017).

NDA Request & College Campus

Faith Ferber was asked by American University to sign an NDA before she could participate in the sex assault hearing. Though her accuser admitted guilt, she was asked for silence (Kingkade, 2016). Additionally, administrations stated that her attacker would be banned from Greek life, but she later found out that his membership in his fraternity continued and the sanction was not enforced. Based on the U.S. Department of Education guidelines, schools and universities can't require NDAs once a case outcome is determined. When schools engage in these practices, it is likely a civil rights violation and Ferber has filed a complaint. Furthermore, the university banned her from the school library because there was a possibility that she would come into contact with her attacker. These guidelines used by American University further victimized Ferber while making false statements about the punishments her attacker would receive. Moreover, the university engaged in DIIS theory—denying Ferber the right to an educational environment free of sex discrimination, inaction with consistent enforcement of sanctions for the offenders and information suppression with the use of an NDA so that unsuspecting students would not be aware of the sexual assaults. Her accuser was ordered to participate in an online sexual harassment training that made it easier for her assailant to complete. During several interactions with administrators, Ferber saw relaxed enforcement of policies. The hearing to determine the punishment was moved from the month of April to October because it was too close to finals. Yet, Ferber was expected to remain silent, and her attacker could resume his Greek life commitments. When universities and colleges become more concerned with liability and the need for NDAs and less concerned with the victim's well-being, we see a culture of information suppression and support for the attacker's privacy. This support sends that message that the victim's needs are less valuable than the accused.

In another disturbing case of a Baylor University Phi Delta Theta president, Jacob Walter Anderson, the prosecutor accepted a plea deal that led to a fine of $400 or $100 for each sexual assault count (Yan and Burnside 2018). It also supported the climate of hypermasculinity (further discussion in chapter 5) on display during the fraternity events.

The victim attended a frat party in 2016 and was drugged by Anderson when she placed her drink down to dance. She became disoriented after several sips of her tainted drink but did not immediately lose consciousness. Eyeing his victim, Anderson followed the victim around the party and encouraged her outside to a secluded area away from party goers. Feeling a loss of her body, Anderson immediately took advantage of his victim by pulling his pants down and putting his penis in her mouth. His careless attitude caused her to choke and when he was unsatisfied, he stood her up against a wall and vaginally penetrated her from behind. She was no longer a virgin after this attack (Associated Press 2018). He later forced his penis into her mouth and when she finally lost consciousness, he left her on the ground, alone. She awoke gagging and choking on her vomit. However, the prosecutor, LaBorde, led the woman to believe that she would seek justice for her and later accepted a controversial plea deal that would reduce the charges against Anderson to unlawful restraint (Yan and Burnside 2018). Furthermore, this "no contest" plea deal did not require Anderson to register as a sex offender, though he received deferred probation and his criminal record was expunged. One of the reasons for the reduced plea deal was that the evidence did not support the woman's claim of substances used to drug her. Ironically, Baylor University, at the time of Anderson's conviction, was enmeshed in litigation associated with several sexual assault allegations attributed to the football team. Judge Strother, in the Anderson case showed leniency in two additional cases of sexual assaults and Baylor University (Associated Press 2018). These convictions resulted in one attacker receiving deferred probation and the payment of the victim's counseling. Another felony conviction would result in 30 days of prison time for a Baylor attacker and the opportunity to serve the prison sentence on the weekends. Baylor was repeatedly accused of ignoring sexual assault claims and some have suggested that the judge and the prosecutor had ties to the university (Associated Press 2018). But some have claimed that this trial was based on class and privilege due to the types of students that attend Baylor with a median family income of $127,500. This outcry was also attributed to the Brock Turner case at Stanford University.

Chanel Miller was sexually assaulted by Brock Turner, a swimmer on the Stanford University team. Both Turner and Miller confessed that each were intoxicated when the assault took place, but Miller stated that she did not remember some of the sequence of the events of the assault because her blood alcohol content level was three times the allowable limit (Lombardo 2016). Turner confesses to digitally penetrating Miller but states that he obtained consent. Yet two Swedish heroes, Carl-Fredrik Arndt and Peter Jonsson witnessed the assault and felt it necessary to intervene to help a clearly incapacitated Miller from further attack (Levy 2016). Arndt & Jonsson found Turner "thrusting his hips" into an unconscious Miller. When Turner ran away, Jonsson tackled him. Turner's blood content level was two times the allowable limit and a jury found him guilty of three counts of felony sexual assault. Chanel submitted a scathing letter that later went viral about the aftermath of her assault and how her dignity, value, and sense of worth was stripped after the night of the assault (Margulies 2016). Although the jury found Turner guilty, Judge Persky believed Turner's account of the events thus reconsidering a long prison sentence, stating that it would "severely impact" Turner's life (Lyons 2016). Persky sentenced Turner to six months in jail in which he served three months due to good behavior. Many believe that the lighter sentencing was based on racism, classism and white privilege (Margulies 2016). White males guilty of sexual assault are less likely to receive long term sentencing, while Black males are more likely to receive mandatory minimums in sexual assault trials. This evidence is supported by the Judge Persky's consideration of the letters of character assessment submitted by Turner's family and friends. Persky did not believe that Turner would be a threat to other people in the future nor that he deserved fourteen years in prison (Margulies 2016). Miller would later reveal her identity one year after Turner's sentencing because she believed the world should know her name and learn of the aftermath of her assault in her memoir (Shapiro 2019). Miller explains that she often turned on all the lights at night, put chairs against her door and kept pepper spray and scissors close by just in case she needed to defend herself. She often panicked when she lost consciousness because it reminds her of her helplessness during the attack. She talks of being humiliated when pictures of her naked body were shown in court, and she is hoping that speaking out will guide the healing of other survivors. Turner appealed the verdict of judgment but was denied, and some people from his hometown in Ohio no longer welcomed him because they are aware of his character. Persky, the judge that provided the lenient sentence, would later be recalled and lose his judgeship. When cases like the Brock Turner and Chanel Miller rape receive media attention, it may influence the underreporting of sexual victimization of young adults who are no longer in college and are industry professionals.

Working Professionals and Sexual Violence

As previously examined, non-college students are four times more likely to be a victim of sexual violence or misconduct (Rape, Abuse, Incest National Network [RAINN] 2020). Factors associated with sexual victimization include negative childhood environments of physical violence and neglect, emotional numbness from post-traumatic stress, substance usage and the inability to recognize risk or develop appropriate boundaries and maladaptive coping strategies, impulse behaviors, and self-blame (Relyea and Ullman, 2017). Also, women that experience intimate partner violence and other forms of abuse (sexual and emotional) may also experience sexual victimization (Fargo, 2009, Campbell, et al., 2011; Relyea and Ullman, 2017). For some survivors that experienced sexual abuse in childhood or adolescence, they may experience revictimization in adulthood (Finkelhor, Ormrod, & Turner, 2007; Fargo, 2009; Papalia, et al, 2017; Relyea and Ullman, 2017). The oral narrative below provides a detailed description of the sexual revictimization of a Michelle, a millennial that recalls several assaults as an adolescent and adult.

Michelle's Story—From Victim to Survivor

Michelle's story begins with the retelling of her most recent sexual assault by her boss, and she explains that it was not her first sexual assault. She recalls two additional attempts of acquaintances that tried to force her to have sex with them. Living in Maryland with her mom, she often spent long hours home alone. She recalls that she was fifteen or sixteen years old at the time. There were very few kids that lived in her neighborhood and the ones that were her age, were boys. So, she would hang out with two boys at either her house or their homes, but there was one day when she was getting dressed to go to work and one of the boys came to her house. When she opened the door, he pushed his way in and went to her bedroom upstairs. Michelle states that her friend was determined to have sex with her. He pulled on her clothes, pushed her down on her bed and she began fighting him off. She stated that the doorbell suddenly rang, and it was the cab driver that she had previously called to take her to work that prevented the completion of the rape.

The cab driver came to the door after honking the horn for her for a long period of time and finally came to door to see if she still needed a cab. It was the doorbell ringing that prevented the attack from becoming rape. her neighbor was not successful, and Michelle threw the boy out the house, finished getting dressed for work, got in the cab, and went to work. Later that day when Michelle was on a break, she disclosed the sexual assault to an older woman. Instead of comfort and support, her co-worker was dismissive and told her, "So what," worse things have happened to others. In this narrative, the coworker denied Michelle the support she needed after the disturbing and shocking event. Additionally, the older woman minimized the magnitude of the sexual assault. Michelle didn't have time to process her assault, she had to get back to work and the reaction from her co-worker influenced Michelle's inaction to disclose the assault to her mother. More important, Michelle did not report the assault to law enforcement, thus suppressing the events and labeling it as inconsequential. She never mentioned the assault to anyone in her family.

Second Assault

Her next assault happened after a night of partying with her friends. She and her girlfriend were hanging out with acquaintances. Her girlfriend had a guy that she was seeing, and the guy invited another friend. It was decided by the group that after the club, they would stop by one of the guys' houses and then they would later go to breakfast. When they got in the house, Michelle and her friend were separated. Her friend went into the bedroom with her boyfriend and Michelle was left with his friend in another room. She did not know the guy but he immediately decided that he was going to have sex with her and began his pursuit.

   He started grabbing at her and she managed to squirm away from him, running around the room, and across the bed in an effort to get away from him. He was much bigger, stronger than her, slightly overweight, and drunk. But she was determined that he wasn't going to catch her. She continued jumping across the bed to keep away from him so that he could not grab her. After several minutes, he became exhausted trying to catch her and collapsed onto the bed—completely passed out. She got out of the room and left the house immediately. Again, Michelle did not tell anyone about the attempted rape, and it would be years later when she and her friend would talk about the events of that night. Once her friend learned what happened, she asked Michelle why she didn't scream or cry out. Michelle didn't think about screaming for help, she simply wanted to stay far away from him so he could not attack her.

Third Assault and Rape

When Michelle was seventeen years old, she was forcibly raped by an old boyfriend. She had not spoken with him in a long time, but he came to her house for a visit. They talked about the past and the current trajectory of each other's lives. Michelle explained her old boyfriend attempted to have sex on this recent visit and although she tried to fight him off, she believed that if she fought too hard, he might hit her and become more aggressive.

So, she gave in so that she wasn't physically hurt. Once she stopped fighting him and he was able to penetrate her with the use of brute strength. He would later find her on Facebook, and she was able to confront him about the assault. However, he was not aware that Michelle considered the attack rape and he apologized for his actions.

Fourth Assault and Rape

At twenty-nine, Michelle had graduated from Columbia University Business School with an MBA and a specialty in sales and marketing. Commuting into New York City from the Bronx, she had a great job working in the public sector conducting site visits of public schools and providing feedback to administrators. She believed she had a great relationship with her boss. He often talked about his wife and their open marriage. His wife was bisexual, and he didn't mind that she had other girlfriends as lovers. One day, he commented that his wife believed Michelle was "attractive." He also explained that his wife did not mind if he had sex with other women. Michelle did not admonish the topic of their conversations and believed him to be harmless. One of the roles of her job required that she travel out of the city to other parts of New York State for site visits of public schools. She, a colleague, and her boss traveled to Albany and were invited to a co-worker's home for a dinner party. Though Michelle did not drink at the dinner party, she, her female colleague, and boss would later leave that party and go to a bar near their hotel for drinks. Michelle explains that she had two beers and her female colleague was also drinking. Both would later leave their drinks unattended with her boss and go to the bathroom. When both returned, they finished their drinks and headed back to the hotel. Once safely back at the hotel, their boss invited both women to his room. Michelle states that her colleague sat on the bed with their boss and Michelle sat on the other bed alone. The last thing that she can remember was losing consciousness and "blacking out." When she awoke, it was approximately 3:00 a.m. in the morning, her pants and panties had been removed and her boss was on top of her digitally penetrating her vagina with his fingers. She pushed him off her and he profusely began to apologize stating he thought she was his wife. Ignoring this, Michelle realized that her glasses were missing. She asked him if he knew where her glasses were and if he could help her look for them. She also asked him to help her find her underwear and pants. She did not find her underwear or glasses but left the hotel room once she retrieved her pants and slung them over her shoulder. When she got on the elevator without any clothes on below her waist, a hotel maintenance worker asked her if she was okay. She said she was and took the elevator up three floors to her room. Attempting to get a recounting of the night's events, she called her colleague asking her when she left the room, and her colleague, equally bewildered, stated that she did not know when she left their bosses hotel room, how she got back to her room, how her clothes were removed, or when she got in bed. Michelle would later go to her colleague's hotel room to discuss the timeline but found her boss in the room with her colleague and she left immediately.

Michelle would try to put the events out of her mind and attempt to conduct business by attending the site visit later that morning, but she immediately became light-headed and nauseous, vomiting at the site and left in a cab approximately thirty minutes after arrival. She went to a nearby hospital to receive a rape kit evaluation.

However, the hospital staff treated her like a drug addict when Michelle asked for a drug test and would not conduct the rape kit in order to collect evidence. She told the staff that she believed that she had been sexually assaulted, but they refused to follow standard protocol for sexual assault and rape victims. When she asked that they call the cops, they refused. Michelle would leave the hospital without receiving any help or have any attempts to collect evidence thwarted because of the negligence of the hospital staff. The actions of the hospital staff can easily be attributed to the DIIS theory. Michelle was denied a sexual assault kit examination and showed inaction when the staff refused to contact law enforcement. Furthermore, the information that could be collected from the DNA evidence and data from the drug test could not be provided based upon the staff's response to Michelle's pleas for assistance. She immediately went to the nearest precinct to report the rape.

The cops were much more helpful and cooperative and took a full report of the events and the actions of the hospital. Michelle would demand the arrest and prosecution of her boss and immediately alerted her job about the rape. She returned to work and her boss was placed on suspension pending an investigation. The detectives visited her office several times to interview all who were present during the incident. However, her colleague could not provide any information because she did not remember any of the events because she also "blacked out." After the job's investigation was conducted, the administrators called Michelle into Human Resources to discuss the potential return of her boss to his role and that she would eventually have to work with him again. The organization decision to reinstate Michelle's boss to his previous position and the requirement that the working relationship be re-established shows their blatant disregard and potential to create a hostile work environment for Michelle. But the prosecution's decision to arrest her boss for the sexual assault prevented Michelle from the humiliation of working with her perpetrator. It was this knowledge that prompted her job to fire her boss. But it was clear that if Michelle hadn't reported the rape to law enforcement and pursued prosecution, she would be forced to continue working with her assaulter. Because the hospital refused to collect evidence less than twenty-four hours after the assault, her boss was prosecuted for a lesser charge of sexual assault and received a fine (Phipps, 2018). He pled guilty to the charges, provided a public apology, and lost his job. She has never seen him again. Both institutions failed to support and protect Michelle and she would later leave the job in less than six months after the incident and a legion of co-workers that did not believe her account of the sexual assault.

The rape would seriously damage Michelle's once strong sense of self. She immediately began experiencing social anxiety. She feared crowds, she feared all men, or anyone that came too close to her. She was afraid to leave her home and worse, her husband blamed her for the rape because he had previously warned her that her boss "wanted" her. Michelle describes the "blacking out" as torture because she said she no longer had solace when she closed her eyes to sleep. Because the rape happened when she was unconscious, she could no longer sleep comfortably. She lost weight because she wasn't eating, and she could not find a safe path back to the woman she used to be. She sought help with hypnosis and in one session successfully began to put the pieces of her life back together, learning to feel comfortable when she closed her eyes.

Although she is strong and empowered, she often wonders about an alarming statistic that states you are thirty-five times more likely to be sexually assaulted if you have been assaulted in the past. Her previous assaults infamously mark her as vulnerable and she is afraid that a new predator may "sniff" her out. It's as if survivors carry scars that only predators can see and later single them out for future assault. She does not want the statistic to be true to for her. All news reports of sexual assaults and rapes trigger her back to her previous assaults and these events have forever changed her ideas of safety and identity.

While Michelle believes that she was sexually assaulted twice in her life, after the recounting of each of these attempts, all would be considered sexual assaults based on the 2013 definition of sexual assault and rape. One reason is because of the physical force and intention of the assailants. The forcible penetration of her ex-boyfriend and boss would be instances of rape. But the others are considered sexual assaults. Michelle has made great strides to put her past behind her. She has begun speaking out about her experiences in order to raise awareness about acquaintance rape and after watching the way the #MeToo redefined the feminist movement (Margulies 2016), Michelle believes that women have become empowered after the trauma of assault and rape.

How #MeToo Encourages Societal Accountability

Prominent women in power have begun stepping forward to publicly discuss their victimization and trauma from sexual assaults thus shifting the perspectives of a much-needed national call to action for policy change. Senator Martha McSally "was raped by a superior officer" while she served her country as an Air Force pilot (Stewart 2019). Rising to the rank of commander, McSally became prey to a predator that would later rape her. A crime that she did not report for many years. In this case the intrapsychic perceptions can be applied to DIIS theory of denial, inaction, and information suppression. She came forward to "empower survivors" that they can overcome the dark days following victimization. More important, she spoke out against the pervasive problem of sexual assault in the military and the problematic procedures that made coming forward feel as if the "system was raping (her) all over again" (Ducharme 2019). To date, the Department of Defense has not successfully addressed the the rape and sexual assault culture in the military (Stead Sellers and Lamothe 2019). In 2014, there were approximately 20,300 documented cases that included "rape, forcible sodomy, and groping," in 2016, the number of sexual assault reports reduced to 14,900 with 43 percent of these cases reported by females and 17 percent reported by males. However, in 2018, the number of cases returned to 20,500. While Senator McSally believes that women should continue to serve in the military and does not feel that "keeping women out of the military" is the optimal solution, the issue of sexual violence is pervasive (Ducharme 2019). But this was not the first time that Senator McSally was sexually assaulted. McSally explains that she was sexually assaulted by a high school coach (Stewart 2019) and believes that sexual assault in and outside the military is "abhorrent and intolerable" (Stead Sellers and Lamothe 2019). Her revelations came two months after her colleague, Senator Joni Ernst disclosed that she was raped by someone she was dating in college but never reported the crime or pursued prosecution (North 2019). Her shame, embarrassment and inability to explain what happened was the reason she did not report her victimization, but she did call a campus hotline.

Ernst served in the National Guard in Kuwait and in the U.S. Senate since 2015 after her retirement as a lieutenant colonel. She has supported bills that ask for sexual assault prevention training for all military personnel and states on that our society support "zero tolerance" for sexual assault and "develop and enforce" policies that prevent these crimes (Joni Ernst United States Senator for Iowa n.d.). Yet these powerful female lawmakers' stories do not sound different from the voices and cries of sexual violence in many communities. Both women reported shame, guilt, embarrassment, and confusion after the trauma, a behavior that is associated with denial or control of the assault and the powerlessness each felt after the sex crime. Neither immediately reported their attack and disclosure of the rape did not happen until years later. Inaction and information suppression can also be attributed to both McSally and Ernst. Although McSally experienced backlash when she reported her superior officer, the outcome is not quite different from the multitude of others that have reported retaliation and harsh consequences from corporations for speaking out or violating a non-disclosure agreement.

Celebrities Fuel #MeToo

Rose McGowan states that she was raped by Harvey Weinstein at the Sundance Film Festival and settled with the mogul for $100,000 in 1997 (Elber 2018). But the settlement did not include a non-disclosure agreement and when McGowan went public on Twitter about the rape (identifying Weinstein), litigation ensued. With allegations from several celebrities surfacing about decades of sexual violence at the hands of Weinstein. McGowan turned down a one million dollar offer to sign a non-disclosure agreement about the Sundance rape (Nyren 2017). Pending litigation from Weinstein forced McGowan to sell her home to fight "the monster." Nevertheless, the national discourse that McGowan sparked after her allegations of rape by Weinstein has fueled the #MeToo movement and empowered others to speak out against powerful men in many industries (Elber 2018). When asked by a reporter if McGowan believed herself a warrior, she simply stated "I'm really just trying to stop international rapists and child molesters." The tactics used by Weinstein and his lawyer further support the application of DIIS theory of denial, inaction, and information suppression in order to protect Weinstein and reduce offender blameworthiness associated with focal concerns theory.

McGowan was the subject of a "gaslighting" tactics memo that exposed well-known California attorney, Lisa Bloom intentions to protect Weinstein. Once a litigator for sexually harassed and assaulted victims, Bloom sent a detailed memo to Weinstein in which many call the "dirtbag's handbook," a step-by-step list of instructions to keep the powerful men in power and undermine the victim (Shendruk and Ossola 2019). First, Bloom suggests that McGowan is a "pathological liar." This act can be identified as denial of the facts and disputing McGowan's sexual assault based on DIIS theory. Inaction is displayed by both Bloom and Weinstein when she does not advise Weinstein to admit his guilt and deeds for accountability. Next, she discredits other women that she has represented and suggests the victims start out as "bold" but later the "lies" appear. Bloom further insults McGowan by suggesting she has nothing else happening in her career but her "diatribes" and "online rants." With her first tactic, she proposes befriending McGowan with an intermediary and finding out "what she wants" for a "win-win." Then, she recommends the use of well-placed articles that suggest that McGowan is "unglued." Cease and desist letters, the threat of a lawsuit are attempts applicable to DIIS theory as information suppression and a public announcement with Weinstein and Bloom that announces their alliance could help to quash future attacks regarding sexual misconduct. Bloom advised Weinstein to show his support for current social movements by starting a foundation that supports gender equality or create the Weinstein Standards that require filmmakers to promote more parity or pair up with women's group. Last, Bloom explains that Weinstein's reputation depicted on internet searches is "obnoxious" and he needs help with the clean-up. She further explains that she is well connected with the top firm that can help change the negative portrayal of his reputation and suggests the use of a secure server in order to avoid hacking (Kantor and Twohey 2019).

Ashley Judd and Gwyneth Paltrow Pivotal Role

In a 2015 article, Ashley Judd reports on the sexual misconduct that she experienced from Harvey Weinstein while working on "Kiss the Girls (Setoodeh 2015)." She explicitly maps out the levels of grooming that Weinstein used to harass and coerce her which included inviting her to his hotel room and the suggestion that she "watch [him] shower." She repeatedly turned down his sexual advances that began with the suggestion to help him pick out his clothes. When she is finally able to escape the room after continued attempts by Weinstein to dominate and control an overwhelmed Judd, she begins to blame, shame, and guilt herself and alleged that she was later blackballed by Weinstein and discredited as a "nightmare to work with" (Saad 2019) But she knew she had to tell her story and believed that there would be others that shared similar experiences with Weinstein. She embarked on a journey to raise awareness and by doing so she would regain her power that he stripped from her in that hotel room (Setoodeh 2015). Gwyneth Paltrow would also come forward with similar experiences reported by Judd.

At twenty years old, Weinstein would use his power and privilege to coerce Paltrow to come into his hotel suite for a "work meeting" and later "massages" (Abrams and Kantor 2017). Brad Pitt, her boyfriend at the time, would later confront Weinstein about his behavior, but Paltrow believed that coming forward to tell her story would end the reign of powerful men that disenfranchised unsuspecting women. She stated, "this way of treating women ends now!" The #MeToo movement and the Weinstein allegations began the societal accountability era linked to the offender blameworthiness of the intersectionality of powerful, wealthy men. It also brought victimized men out of the shadows.

Anthony Rapp and Kevin Spacey

In 1986, Anthony Rapp was fourteen and attends a party at Kevin Spacey's apartment (Gajanan 2018). At the end of the night, Rapp explains that Spacey escorts him to his bedroom and "climbs on top of him." Spacey does not remember the incident, of course. Remembering the incident would suggest the illegality of the sexual misconduct because Rapp was underage. But Rapp came forward with the allegations because he saw the "impact" that the #MeToo movement had garnered and considered that people "can be believed" when telling their stories of sexual misconduct, assault and rape. Rapp described the influence of the social movement as a "sea change" and that predators could no longer escape the allegations of their sexual improprieties. What the #MeToo movement has done is shine a light on the need for accountability of sexual predators and their enablers who are complicit in the cover up. As a result of Rapp's allegations, Kevin Spacey lost his recurring lead role on the Netflix show *House of Cards*, and his role in and upcoming Ridley Scott film (Clarke 2018). Rapp believed that Says "there is strength in numbers."

Conclusion

While the #MeToo continues to expose the predatory nature of powerful well-known celebrities and industry professionals, the prevalence of sexual violence and victimization continues to grow. The application of denial, in- action, and information suppression can easily be applied to countless cases involving teens and young adults in which educational institutions have ignored Title IX guidelines and engaged in methods that blame and shame victims while hiding the details of the sex crime with non-disclosure and confidentiality agreements. The attacker actions are kept secret and may not prosecuted. Moreover, factors associated with negative home environments, past abuse and trauma, substance usage, risk taking behavior and the inability to detect unsafe social environments may lead to future re-victimization in adulthood. Chapter 5 will explore the motivations of the offender and the psychological aftermath that victims face when attempting to overcome the trauma associated with sex violence.

CHAPTER FIVE

~

Applications of DIIS Theory to the Psyche of the Victim and Offender

Intersectionality plays an important role in a sexually violent crime. Gender, race, ethnicity, age, class, privilege, and culture are some of the factors that may concern a victim of this type of trauma and can be attributed to an offender (Christensen and Harris 2019). Within the framework of the focal concerns theory is:

a. An offender's blameworthiness
b. The desire to protect the community from threat
c. Imposition of constraints and consequences that result in convictions

And elements of DIIS theory of denial, inaction, and information suppression can be associated with the intrapsychic perceptions of both the victim and perpetrator before, during, and after the occurrence of a sexual assault (Tillman et al., 2010). The purpose of this chapter is the application of DIIS theory in order to examine various forms of psychological dysfunction that is attributed to the survivor, the aftermath of the sexual assault (Campbell & Fehler-Cabral, 2018) and the offender's selection of a vulnerable target. Societal institutions reluctance to provide consequences for the offender and prosecution while victim blaming and the use of non-disclosure aggrements will also be assessed and applied to DIIS theory.

Surviving the Sex Assault: The Aftermath

Recalling the events of the intimate violation, the possibility of physical scars and bruises, and the psychological distress and shock (Haskell and Randall, 2019; Villalta, et al., 2020) can be attributed to denial, inaction, and information suppression. There are a myriad of questions that are formulating in a person's mind that survives sexual violence (Tillman, et al., 2010). The powerlessness and loss of control linked with the freeze response of immobility and shock is associated with the ways a victim "denies" their ability to control or comprehend the sexual violation of their body by a trusted friend, acquaintance, or family member. Psychologically, the victim may dissociate from their body when experiencing pain and injury from the unwanted penetration of their genital regions (i.e., anus, vagina) (World Health Organization 2003). Dissociation and emotional numbness (Burgess, 2018; Haskell and Randall 2019) may occur as a direct and indirect outcome of the trauma (Lahav, Ginzburg and Spiegel 2019). When sexual violence occurs, it is one crime in which survivors may exhibit reluctance because of self-blame, victim shaming and ridicule (McLaughlin, 2019; Papalia, Mann and Ogloff, 2020). Before the victim seeks help or reports the incidence, emotional numbness may begin (Burgess 2018). This happens as a result of dissociation. When a person is sexually assaulted it is an uncontrollable physical attack that threatens one's safety (Haskell and Randall 2019). The fight or flight defense responses kick in but if the victims are overpowered by the strength of the attacker and feels threat of death, the "mind leaves the body" through dissociation as a form of survival until the violence ends. PTSD symptoms are more prevalent when dissociation occurs (DeCou, et al. 2017). Additionally, victims are more likely to experience PTSD symptoms if they receive negative support (i.e., victim shaming, blaming and ridicule) after the disclosure of the trauma. The symptoms of PTSD can be placed into four categories (a) intrusive thoughts, (b) avoidance, (c) negative thoughts, and (d) hyperarousal (American Psychiatric Association, 2017; Haskell and Randall; Villalta, et al, 2020)

Psychological distress, depression, and self-blame increase when there are negative social reactions and responses (Haskell and Randall, 2019; Villalta, et al, 2020). For example, when rumors or a video about the sexual assault are distributed via social media, *intrusive thoughts*, recurring dreams and memories of the event surface. The inability to focus or attend to meaningful daily routines become problematic. *Avoidance* of other people or similar places that may make the victim feel unsafe or remind the victim of the assault can trigger distress. It is not uncommon for a victim to withdraw from the activi-

ties that once provided happiness in order to regain control, a sense of security, and a pathway to survive (Haskell and Randall, 2019). *Negative feelings*
about ways that the victim could have avoided the sex assault or could have
foreseen the motives of the attacker surface. They feel responsible, internal-
ize the negative beliefs by increasing their negative self-talk (i.e., I'm stupid
or dumb, I should have known he would hurt me, etc.) and show signs of
hyperarousal (Rentoul and Appleboom 1997). Sensory triggers become daily
occurrences that cause sleepless nights, intense fear and terror, anxiety and
panic that simulate a racing heart, palpitations, sweats, and the inability to
breathe. For victims that suffer repeated acts of sexual abuse, they experience
continued trauma stress (CTS) (Eagle and Kaminer 2013). This psychological distress is long lasting because of the notion that further victimization
is imminent and uncontrollable. It intensifies the development of mental
health issues in the future. It also adds to the internalization of the "negative
judgment from others, self-evaluations of embarrassment and inferiority"
which can further be described as "social threat."

Depression

The sense of sadness and worthlessness is overwhelming when your body is
violated (Cassada Lohmann and Raja 2016). Some of the most significant
foundations of identity are shattered during the crime of a sexually violent
act (Rentoul and Appleboom 1997). But identity after a sexual assault is
much different for men than women. Men experience threats to their mascu-
line identity. Trust and intimacy boundaries are obliterated for both females
and males (Choudhary, Smith, and Bossarte 2012). Feeling helpless and the
inability to feel happy or pleasure (anhedonia) becomes more common and
suicidal thoughts surface (Rentoul & Apple boom, 1997; Haskell and Randall, 2019). But a bodily attack can leave victims lethargic, disoriented and
exhausted for weeks which can be associated with post-traumatic stress disorder (Choudhary, Smith and Bossarte 2012). They may feel dirty and unclean
and may spend hours trying to scrub the invisible dirt off their body. Some
may struggle to identify coping skills that work effectively to increase value,
reduce flashbacks, or support healthier eating habits. This is considered inaction because a survivor may not seek help or utilize the community resources
for survivors of sexual assault (i.e., seek medical attention, receive a rape kit,
counseling) (Tillman, et al. 2010). Depression can be combated with a loving supportive network of friends and family that know the importance of
validation. Early established support networks are instrumental in reducing

the long-term effects of PTSD, reducing signs of depression and substance dependency (Gravelin, Biernat, and Buche 2019).

Many people often question the motives of survivors of sexual violence when they delay the disclosure of the sexual victimization (Rentoul and Appleboom 1997). Telling someone that you were raped or sexually assaulted is *never* easy and there are several factors that must be considered before a person feels safe enough to confide in another person about this intimate violation (Broman-Fulks, et al. 2007). These factors include (RAINN 2019):

- the relationship to the offender
- the status of the offender
- possible substance usage
- the age of the victim
- the details of the assault
- timing and context of the disclosure
- the threat of disclosure from the perpetrator
- the reaction of the person that first learns of the sexual assault
- the psychological well-being and mental health of the victim
- available resources for the victim

Victim and Survivor

There is a societal debate regarding the use of the words victim or survivor of sexual assault (Muldoon, Taylor, and Norma 2016). The sheer ugliness of one of the most intimate violations of your body without consent and the racing thoughts that go through your mind before, during, and after the rape must be explored. The rape is a trauma that affects all aspects of:

- Mind: self-identity, shame, guilt, blame, how others may now perceive you and your future potential for happiness
- Body: personal security, sense of safety, body image, dress behavior
- Spirit: shattered beliefs, faith, optimism

Both words apply at different stages of realization and acknowledgement (Augustine 2019). First, the victims must come to terms with the fact that she was selected by the sexual predator. She was not aware that she was singled out and become prey. Statistics show that the predator is someone you know (RAINN 2019). In approximately 70 percent of rapes (seven out of ten), the predator knows the victim. 93 percent of children or teen victims know their abuser.

The perpetrator was most likely an undetected rapist in the community that secretly looked for opportunities to increase the number of his sexual conquests (Lisak and Miller 2002). These predators are often hypersexed, hypermasculine, and show little or no regard for their prey. They have distorted and antiquated views of women and don't have family or friends that challenge their belief system or sexual proclivities (California Coalition Against Sexual Assault 2017). Each assault is an orgasmic reward that can easily create an addiction.

The Oxford dictionary defines a *victim* as someone that has been "harmed, injured, or killed as a result of a crime, accident, or other event or action." Additionally, a victim can be "duped or tricked or has come to feel helpless and passive in the face of misfortune or ill-treatment." For the rape victim, all of these examples are true and applicable.

In order to report rape, you must feel empowered, strong, and fearless (Sheley 2018). Male sexual assault survivors are least likely to report the crime Rentoul & Appleboom, 1997; Monk-Turner & Light, 2010). In this society, trashing the victimized and traumatized is a negative response often used by people that don't know how to respond to rape. Some choose to deny, ridicule, and bash the survivors (Tinkler, Becker, and Clayton 2018). But worse, communities of strangers ignore the severity of sexual violence if the assault does not cause physical injury or worse, call the victims liars (Boyle and Walker 2016). These are forms of denial which can be indicators of the potential for inaction and information suppression.

There are cases where mothers don't believe molested and raped children (Adams, 1994) and family members, friends, and co-workers, admonish victims because the predator is often someone in power or beloved in the community: a loving son, winning coach, rich businessman, dignified prosecutor, trusting sports doctor, or virtuous judge (California Coalition Against Sexual Assault 2017). Intersectionality plays a role in offender blameworthiness and societal attribution of accountability and appropriate consequences, potential prosecution, and conviction (Sheley 2018). The Oxford dictionary defines a *survivor* as "a person who survives, especially a person remaining alive after an event in which others have died or a person who copes well with difficulties in their life."

As the victim develops a new sense of self and creates a stronger sense of identity, they seek help, counseling, and support from others (Campbell, et al. 2015). But for some, this may take years (even decades) to rebuild their spiritual connectedness to their bodies. They slowly put all the pieces back together, admit to themselves that they were once a victim, but have survived the ordeal. It is at this point that they may decide to tell another person or possibly report the ordeal they survived. However, male survivors of sexual assault have different psychological experiences and help seeking motivations (Monk-Turner and Light 2010). In a study of 219 males that were sexually assaulted, the likelihood of seeking counseling was approximately 29 percent, with 81 percent who avoided help seeking resources. The findings posited that males that were sexually assaulted and penetrated experienced self-blame, shame and humiliation which prevented them from seeking help.

Societal and Cultural Blaming of the Sex Assault Victim

In order to address the social and cultural hurdles associated with blaming the victim, we must return to the gender scripts produced by the patriarchal society in which we live (Gravelin, Biernat, and Buche 2019). As a society, we are more likely to blame the victim of sexual assault as a result of acquaintance rape (when a victim knows the attacker) than stranger rape (Boyle & Walker, 2016; Campbell & Fehler-Cabral, 2018). Moreover, minimization and denial of the sexual assault is associated with the severity of the assault (physical force, bruising, and use of a weapon) and victimization by a stranger (Boyle and Walker 2016). Additionally, a prevalence of gender differences exists when assigning blame and accountability in sexually violent situations. In America, males are expected to have advanced knowledge and a larger number of sexual experiences than their female counterparts. They are also expected to initiate sex, control the setting, and dictate the terms of the act. For example, males are more likely to blame victims in settings where drinking and substances are used for sexual coercion (i.e., frat parties). The hypermasculine narrative encourages male dominance and power thus resulting in the label of males as sexual aggressors. Reports of aggressive predators on college campuses working in tandem are part the zeitgeist. This can be seen with several fraternities' dismissal from campus.

Phi Delta Theta was kicked off their Texas Tech University in 2014 for hosting a party that included a sign that stated, "No Means Yes, yes Means Anal." (Kingkade 2014). In 2016, the Yale fraternity Delta Kappa Epsilon was reinstated after a five-year ban when members were identified in a video chanting misogynistic profanities against women which stated:

My name is Jack, I'm a necrophiliac, I f— dead women, And fill them with my semen, No means yes, Yes means anal . . . F—ing sluts, F—ing sluts, USA, USA

With the disrespectful tone of this profane song, it's not hard to see why young women are taking back their power.

Fighting Back

It is not uncommon for young women to warn each other about the potential harm of sexual violence at frat parties with messages of names of student predators on bathroom walls (Culp-Ressler 2014). A sexual assault report released by the University of Texas-Austin campus in 2017 showed that 15 percent of undergraduate girls were raped and 32 percent did not report the crime to law enforcement (Stone 2017). A rape list was created on the "Make Them Scared" website of suspected offenders on the University of Washington campus. The list included approximately four hundred names (Fields 2016). In 2015, Emma Sulkowicz carried a blue mattress to classes and various places on the Columbia University campus in order to protest her disagreement with the university's decision to allow her alleged assaulter, Paul Nungesser, to remain on campus and complete his studies after a consensual sex encounter became violent (Morabito 2017). Although investigations of the sexual assault were conducted by both Columbia University and the New York Police Department, Nungesser was cleared of all wrongdoing and recently settled with Columbia University for an undisclosed amount because the university was accused of allowing one student to slander another student. Sulkowicz became nationally known as "mattress girl" and regaled by women across the country for her stand against Columbia University and Nungesser's alleged violence. She was invited by Sen. Kristen Gillibrand to the 2015 State of the Union address and received the Susan B. Anthony award and identified as a Women of Courage in 2016. Nungesser, though exonerated, will always be known as the man that attacked "mattress girl." With the #MeToo movement, American women have exposed the previous undetected rapists and the ways non-disclosure agreements are used to silence their experiences for information suppression (Smith 2019). But what about the invisible cloak or shroud that hides the unknown sex offenders? More importantly, can undetected rapists be a result of the current zeitgeist of hypermasculinity, hostile sexism and the focal concern of the lack of offender blameworthiness in American rape culture?

Are We Raising Undetected Rapists?

As Americans, there is huge controversy associated with the idea that we are raising rapists (Orlando 2016). And that once raised, we ignore the behaviors, rarely penalize the perpetrators, and often feel uncomfortable discussing the topic. These are the early indicators of DIIS theory (denial, inaction, information suppression). Some blame the political correctness of our national conversations but recently, there has been a rise in the number of reports of sexual assaults perpetrated by powerful legislators, athletes, entertainers, Hollywood producers, and others (Almukhtar, Gold and Buchanan 2018). But what are the factors that can create the psyche where rape is an option? More important, does a rapist believe they have committed a crime? Past research may provide answers regarding the intrapsychic experiences of undetected rapists.

One of the most widely cited studies was conducted in 2002 in Boston, Massachusetts by Lisak and Miller. This seminal study explored the sexual behaviors of 1,882 male students at an urban commuter college in Massachusetts and laid the foundation for the current zeitgeist associated with undetected rapes, repeat rapists and the positive correlation with interpersonal violence. Lisak and Miller (2002) found that many of the males' rape behavior went undetected and was not prosecuted. Additionally, it was found that these males were "repeat rapists" where the majority of the men engaged in interpersonal violence.

Rape crimes are rarely reported to authorities (approximately 64 percent to 96 percent of rapes committed are not reported), it was astonishing to learn that these participants did not consider their actions "criminal" in nature (Lisak and Miller, 2002). Most perpetrators do not believe that they have committed a crime and their denial is associated with sexual recidivism rates (Langton, et al. 2008). Lisak & Miller (2002) reported that of the 1,882 men surveyed regarding sexual practices that included forms of rape and interpersonal violence, approximately 80 percent of sexually assaulted victims who were incapacitated and under the influence of drugs or alcohol. However, many males would not consider this or identify this as rape. The illuminating truth of this study is that approximately 63 percent of the men were considered repeat rapists. While critics of this study believe that the serial predation of rape can't be generalized to all college campuses (Swartout, et al. 2015), it is important to examine the psyche of the men committing this crime. If you don't believe you have committed rape, you are more likely to repeat the use of power, manipulation, and control during sexual acts when reprimands and consequences are absent. This application of DIIS theory (denial, inaction, and information suppression) can be attributed to the power dynamic and the focal concern of offender blameworthiness.

Lisak and Miller (2002) further purported that 9.2 percent of participants used threats of, or overt force, to coerce sex with 10 percent using the same methods to coerce oral sex. The horror of these findings is that these are "undetected rapes." Men that have committed the crime and were not charged. Of the 1,882 participants of the study, seventy-six identified as repeat rapists (committing two or more rapes) who committed approximately five rapes for a total of 439 rapes. In this study, it was apparent that a positive correlation existed between the increasing number of undetected rapists and the number of rapes committed. Denial led to increased sexual victimization. The researchers were able to identify the undetected rapists with the use of self-reporting questionnaires. Lisak and Miller (2002) used clever tactics with the formulations of the questions. By omitting negatively charged words like rape from the questions, the participants provided "yes" responses to the following questions:

1. Have you ever been in a situation where you tried, but for various reasons did not succeed, in having sexual intercourse with an adult by using or threatening to use physical force (twisting their arm, holding them down, etc.) if they did not cooperate?
2. Have you ever had sexual intercourse with someone, even though they did not want to, because they were too intoxicated (on alcohol or drugs) to resist your sexual advances (e.g., removing their clothes)?
3. Have you ever had sexual intercourse with an adult when they didn't want to because you used or threatened to use physical force (twisting their arm; holding them down, etc.) if they didn't cooperate?
4. Have you ever had oral sex with an adult when they didn't want to because you used or threatened to use physical force (twisting their arm; holding them down, etc.) if they didn't cooperate?

Additionally, these answers were obtained because the researchers provided anonymity and confidentiality agreements that would not result in reports to law enforcement agencies or criminal investigations of the men. But what about the survivors of these 439 rapes? Did these men feel remorse, regret, guilt or shame for the behavior toward their victims? Unfortunately, these types of questions were not included in the survey.

Distrubingly, Lisak, and Miller (2002) found that the majority of these rapists also engaged in other forms of interpersonal violence against partners and/or physical and sexual abuse of children. Thus, providing a deeper connection to the type of person that commits rape would also commit other violations and crimes against humanity. When addressing the issue of undetected rapists, what are some of the intrapsychic factors that many of these perpetrators possess?

Intrapsychic Selection of Victims

One of the reasons why rapists are undetected is the selection of the victim. They engage in acquaintance rape and often know their victims (Lisak, 2002). One example can be associated with the Nate Parker case.

Nate Parker is a well-known actor, writer, director, and producer. During the lead up to the release of his film "Birth of a Nation," information surfaced about a 2001 rape trial in which Nate Parker and his roommate Jean Celestin were the defendants (Pearl 2016). The details of the alleged rape, its aftermath, and the appeals after the trial may have led to the suicide of the victim in 2012.

In the summer of 1999, Parker and the victim meet through a mutual friend. She likes him and invites him to her dorm room where they kiss and though Parker attempts to have sex with her, she stops him and performs oral sex on him (Pearl 2016). Before the encounter ends, they schedule a date to meet in at a neighborhood bar. While waiting at the bar, the victim has too many cocktails with other patrons until Parker shows up for the date (he was two hours late). Seeing her drunken state, Parker encouraged her to sleep at his place—giving her his bed while he slept on the couch. She agrees that she is too drunk to return to her dorm room and falls asleep in Parker's bed. Later she awakes to Parker having sex with her through bouts of consciousness. She also remembers, though vaguely that she had sex with Celestin. Most of the details of the rape are blurred because she was not conscious to provide consent. Several weeks after the incident, she gets examined by a doctor and seeks counseling. She later reports the incident to the police and the young men are charged with rape and kicked off the wrestling team. She also reports the incident to the university. Parker and Celestin begin stalking and harassing the victim after she goes to the police with the allegations. As a result of the intimidation, the accuser makes her first suicide attempt. The trial continues and although Nate Parker would later be acquitted because he had a prior sexual relationship with the accuser, his roommate was found guilty and sentenced. Both were expelled from Penn State University after the trial and Celestin would later make two appeals, but the last appeal would get thrown out because the accuser refused to testify. Sadly, in 2012, Parker and Celestin's accuser would commit suicide by overdosing on sleeping pills. This case has many of the remnants and details of acquaintance and nonconsensual rape, but with a tragic ending.

Knowing the victim is ideal for the rapists because these types of victims are less likely to report the assault because of fear of reprisal from the rapist, the interrogation during the legal process, and others in the community becoming aware of the sexual assault. It is not uncommon for communities, families, and friends to engage in the "blame the victim" syndrome (Sampson 2013). But they have also selected a method that makes their acquaintance vulnerable (Lisak, 2008). This includes selecting a potential victim and experimenting with his/her boundaries. These undetected rapists will determine what boundaries can be crossed or how much coercion may be used to blur the boundary line. They will target a victim and devise the tactics that will be used to "physically isolate" and instigate the assault. Like a cheetah hunting down a vulnerable gazelle or impala, the undetected rapists will not stop until the conquest is won or the rape completed.

Belief Systems and Behaviors

Most undetected predators are more sexually active than others and their psyche drives them to believe that if they are not having sex, then their masculinity will suffer (Lisak, 2002). More importantly, they have a warped sense of beliefs about the sexual behaviors of men and women. They often believe in the traditional masculine/feminine ideals. These stereotypes associated with the rape myth suggest that "no really means yes" and that women are a sexual conquest. Their belief that they need to control, manipulate, and exert power from consenting and nonconsenting sexual partners is a common thought loop on repeat in their minds. For example, if a victim begins to deny the predator sex, his goal may shift to domination with force or the threat of force. Alcohol is a tool and tactic widely used by rapists. Drugs are also useful to incapacitate an unsuspecting victim (Lisak, 2008). An unconscious victim is easier to assault and needs less restraint, physical aggression, or force (Kingkade, 2017). One example of the use of substances and a list of unconscious victims can be attributed to the allegations against Bill Cosby.

Bill Cosby

Bill Cosby, everyone's favorite TV dad helped change the image of the black family in the 1990s with "The Cosby Show." He enjoyed a formidable career that has spanned over six decades and can boast a record number of achievements and well-deserved awards. Yet those accomplishments coincide with allegations of rape and sexual misconduct with sixty women (Kim, Littlefield, and Etehad 2017). According to allegations and Bill Cosby's admission, he has given quaaludes to women he wanted to have sex with and has given these drugs to other people (Holly, McLaughlin, and Ford 2015). Additionally, Cosby admitted in a 2005 deposition that he obtained at least seven prescriptions from a (now deceased) Los Angeles gynecologist and cosmetic surgeon named Leroy Amar (Moghe 2015).

Cosby's use of quaaludes or methaqualone was strategic because the drug can be slipped into drinks without detection (King 2017). Unsuspecting victims can't smell or taste the illicit drug. It quickly dissolves in liquid and leaves the person powerless because they experience paralysis, immobility, disorientation, dizziness, and sleep. Like most drugs, quaaludes provide a sense of euphoria (Rhodan 2016) but it also renders the victim unable to give consent to unwanted sexual advances. Off the market since the late 1980s, how was Cosby able to obtain these drugs in 2004? Andrea Constand alleges that America's favorite dad used quaaludes when he raped her at his home in Montgomery, Pennsylvania (Engel 2017). Were these leftover pills that Cosby was unable to use in the late 80s and 90s after quaaludes were taken off the market? Or did he have another supplier? Most accounts of the sixty accusations of sexual misconduct and assault against Cosby include drinks, drugs, and unconsciousness (Olivier 2015). But one account from Carla Ferrigno explains that Cosby attempted to sexually assault her at his Beverly Hill's home in 1967 and she alleges that Camille Cosby may have been complicit (McDonald 2014).

On a double date with Cosby, his wife, and a friend, Ferrigno recounts that the group returned back to Cosby's home for a game of pool. Unlike the other accounts, Ferrigno was not drugged because she repeatedly refused the drinks that Cosby and his friend attempted to give to her. She states that Camille later disappeared and so did her date and she was left alone with Cosby. When she asked where his wife had gone, Cosby stated that he didn't know, and that Camille may have gone to bed. When Ferrigno refused yet another drink, Cosby grabs her and kisses her roughly as she fought him off. He lunges for her, and she manages to tear herself away from him, leaving the room and roaming through the house in which she finds her date and they leave the house. She believes she was lucky, but she adamantly believes that Camille knew all these years about Cosby's sexual proclivities and she did nothing (McDonald 2014).

During a two-day deposition in February 2016 regarding her husband's sexual assault trial, Camille Cosby sites marital privilege as the reason to avoid answering ninety-eight questions in which she defends Cosby's and the communications she had with him about his sexual assault behaviors (Rosenbaum 2016). While many women would love to blame Camille solely, Cosby's complicit community of enablers to his alleged sexual violence spreads far beyond his home. There are countless others that may have participated in helping Cosby use his power to manipulate women. Many have suggested that there were friends that would introduce Cosby to these unsuspecting women knowing his predatory practices.

For example, before his death, Hugh Hefner was deposed and asked to provide testimony of his knowledge of sexual battery in a 1974 and 2008 Playboy mansion visit against Cosby in which Judy Huth, an underage minor in 1974, and Chloe Goins, a former model, were drugged and assaulted (Associated Press 2016). Both women claim that Hefner was complicit and believe that he had prior knowledge of Cosby' s previous sexual exploitation of women at the Playboy Mansion (Gajanan, Bill Cosby's Sex Abuse Cases Ensnare Hugh Hefner 2016). Yet, a former employee working at the Brooklyn studios of the Cosby Show also helped Cosby hide his behavior.

Frank Scotti, a former NBC employee was asked by Cosby to pay off several women with money orders (Stedman 2014). More important, Cosby asked Scotti to put his name on the money orders so that the payment would not lead back to Cosby. Scotti added his name to monthly payments of $2,000 that were sent between 1984–1992 to various women. To support his claims, Scotti produced copies of money orders to four women in which one woman verified that payments helped finance her son's private school tuition. And yet one of the money order copies went to Shawn Thompson, who alleges that she had an affair with Cosby in 1974 and received over $100,000 from Cosby who also fathered her daughter, Autumn Jackson. At the time of this printing, DNA tests were not performed to corroborate the claim. What's most disturbing about the long list of sexual allegations associated with Cosby is not his admission to using illegal sedatives and drugs to slip into drinks of unsuspecting victims, or Camille's feigned ignorance of Cosby's fifty years of alleged sexual assault, nor an NBC employee's statement and evidence of money orders of payments to women Cosby directed him to pay off. But it's the initial public outpouring of support of Cosby's innocence and his resulting 2017 mistrial in which twelve jurors could not agree on his guilt (Chen 2017).

First, when exploring the public outcry, Cosby had a long list of celebrity supporters which included some of the Cosby cast (Rashad, Warner, and Pulliam), Whoopi Goldberg, Jill Scott (though she would later rescind her support), Damon Wayans, and Eddie Griffith (Holloway 2016). Joe Torry, Lewis Dix, Jr., and Sheila Frazer attended the 2017 trial (Lockett 2017). While these celebrities may be able to explain the sheer genius of Bill Cosby's comedic skill, timing, and business acumen, they can't attest to his sexual proclivities nor explain his admission that he used illicit drugs with women he targeted for sex or his years of master criminal activity. Ironically, of the sixty women that have come forward to expose America's favorite dad, there was only one woman that was able to bring the case to trial. Why—when there is such a rich history of Cosby's sexual misconduct?

Maybe it's the fact that in the late 60s and early 70s, the definition for rape was antiquated (Federal Bureau of Investigation Criminal Justice Information Services Division 2013) and the shaming, disbelief, and silencing of victims more likely. Additionally, many states' statutes of limitations prevented these women from pursuing prosecution. On average, most states statutes expire within ten to twelve years or less after the sexual abuse, and/ or assault was committed thus making it harder to prosecute these types of crimes (Reilly 2016). But truthfully, elapsed statutes and a supportive community of people, law enforcement agencies, corporations, and institutions are the real reason why sexual predators thrive. Someone always knows about the deviant practices, abuses, and victims because it is often reported, allegations ignored, and buried under non-disclosure agreements. DIIS theory is systematically relevant to his sexual recidivism. First, Cosby has repeatedly denied the sexual assault accusations and several institutions (i.e., NBC, previous prosecute that would not indict Cosby) inaction attributed to the increasing number of victims. Moreover, non-disclosure agreements contributed to information suppression and public awareness. Payments to the accusers by an NBC employee (instructed by Cosby) helped ensure the silence.

However, the #MeToo movement gained extraordinary momentum as a result of Alyssa Milano's tweet on October 15, 2017, that would lead to justice finally being served to Bill Cosby in April 2018 (Garcia 2017). America's favorite dad was convicted of three counts of indecent assault after he drugged and sexually assaulted Andrea Constance in 2004 (Levenson and Cooper 2018). He is currently serving a sentence of three to ten years (Arkin 2019), but may serve ten years because he refuses to admit his guilt and apologize for his actions (Puente 2019). Yet, this did not prevent him from suing Constand in 2016 for a confidentiality agreement breach. Cosby has never admitted to his predatory actions and was released from jail on June 30, 2021, as a result of a sweetheart binding agreement that was made between him and then district attorney Bruce Castor that he would not be charged with a sex crime (Davis, Katersky, and Hutchinson, 2021). Today, he is a free man, but prosecutors have asked that the U.S. Supreme Court review the Cosby case (Tsioulcas, 2021). The black eye of historical sexual assault by men in powerful positions and the community of people who help the predators thrive was never more apparent than the case of Dr. Larry Nassar, USA Gymnastics and Michigan State University doctor.

Dr. Larry Nassar

On the outset, Dr. Nassar had an illustrious career as a physician working with gymnast and other athletes. He provided treatment to many aspiring Olympians during the twenty-nine years that he worked with the USA Gymnastics program. Additionally, he was well known in the local Michigan gymnast community during his nineteen years on staff at Michigan State University's athletic department, serving girls younger than thirteen years old through adulthood (Connors 2018). But it was his use of "specialized treatment" that consisted of nonconsensual digital penetration without gloves or lubricant of young aspiring gymnasts' vaginas, anuses, while massaging their breasts and worse, raping some of them (Magness 2017). By the time he was brought to justice, he was responsible for the abuse of 332 survivors (Levenson 2018) and exposing community and institutional negligence of both Michigan State University and the USA Gymnastics (BBC 2018). However, the culture of complicity of various institutions uncovered during the investigation and trial of Dr. Nassar was the most damaging. Overall, five institutions were alerted of Dr. Nassar's sexual misconduct with athletes that included (1) Michigan State University, (2) USA Gymnastics, (3) the MSU Police Dept., (4), the Ingraham County Prosecutor's office, and (5) the FBI. With the massive number of complaints against the esteemed physician nearing 332, did Dr. Nassar's devious deeds fall on deaf ears. DIIS Theory can be associated with years of abuse and Nassar's denial that his sex crimes were part of the proposed treatment. The systematic inaction of the five listed institutions and failure to conduct thorough criminal investigations, inform Title IX coordinators, or pursue charges is easily defined as complicity. But the use of non-disclosure agreements and threats of punishment and fines for the victims can be applied to information suppression and victim blame and shame.

During Nassar's 2018 trial, the Meridian Police Department apologized for their negligence when they failed to send police reports of Nassar's sexual assaults to prosecutors (Darrah 2018). In the aftermath of Nassar's sex scandal and trial it was revealed that fourteen officials from Michigan State (administrators, coaches, and trainers) were alerted to Nassar's deplorable fetishes, yet did nothing, thus allowing his confidence to grow and his molestations to continue (Rios 2018). Michigan State University's president resigned, and the former boss of Nassar and dean of Michigan State University's osteopathic medical school, William Strampel stepped down as a result of a criminal investigation against him of sexual misconduct with students, sexual harassment of female students, pornography of MSU female students and sex toys found on his work and home computer. He was dean while Dr. Nassar worked for him and took the post in 2002 (Counts 2018). This may explain why he did not object to Dr. Nassar's practices or report them.

Additionally, the USA Gymnastics board members resigned, and the liabilities associated with this group of adults that failed to act on these young student athletes' and Olympic gymnasts' behalf are finally the subject of investigation (Stateside Staff 2018).

On September 15, 2021, Olympic gymnasts Simone Biles, Aly Raisman, McKayla Maroney, and USA Gymnast Maggie Nichols testified in a televised Senate Judiciary regarding the repeated and long-term sexual abuse they suffered at the hands of Dr. Larry Nassar (Associated Press, 2021). Each woman provided explicit details of their extensive abuse and condemnation of USA Gymnastics and the Federal Bureau of Investigation that failed to prosecute Dr. Nassar. FBI agents took the gymnasts statements but did not indict the team doctor. Their inaction and information suppression led to the sexual victimization of forty young teenage girls. To date, Dr. Nassar victimized approximately three hundred girls and it prompted Simone Biles to question "what is a little girl worth"—during the senate hearing. On December 13, 2021, USA Gymnastics, the U.S. Olympic and Paralympic Committee reached a $380 million dollar settlement for their negligence in protecting the teens and young woman from a known sexual predator (Blistein, 2021). The settlement could likely bankrupt these three institutions that engaged in the three identified steps of DIIS Theory (denial, inaction, and information suppression). The focal concerns theory is also applicable to this case because law enforcement also participated in the DIIS Theory thus exposing their complicity in the sexual assaults of forty new victims. Offender blameworthiness, failure to keep the public safe, and societal cost because they failed to initially prosecute Nassar. If the culture of complicity was not a fully functioning process, most predators would be reported, prosecuted, and eventually locked up. However, when predators like Cosby and Dr. Nassar are confronted with allegations, they often deny the claim and label the accusation as false, and institutions protect them (Ryan 2018).

Although many would like to compare the undetected rapists to incarcerated rapists, there is a distinction between them. Undetected rapists often know their prey and are less likely to use weapons to encourage the rape. They are more likely to use psychological warfare by controlling the rape environment, using isolation, and manipulating the victim's idea of safety and state of consciousness. Their selection of their victims may also be the key factor for their undetection. Incarcerated rapists are more likely to pick strangers; undetected rapists select friends and acquaintances (Lisak, 2002).

Undetected rapists are more dangerous than their incarcerated counterparts because in consequence-free sexual assault situations, getting away with crime leads to the possibility of more attempts. The lack of consequence becomes a positive reinforcer to rapists because of the:

1. future selection of a specific type of victim
2. methods used
3. correlation of the sexual orgasmic release as a reward, thus making the need for this form of pleasure more likely

In spite of everything we know about sexual assault and rape, the creepiest statistics that makes my hair standup on the back of my neck is that out of one thousand rapes, 994 will not get arrested, or see jail time for their crime (Rape, Abuse, and Incest National Network 2018). This means that there are more undetected rapists terrorizing local communities and scaring enough of their victims so that they won't report the rape. They are our family members, friends, neighbors, co-workers, customers, clients, or potential dates. If we are are to determine the root cause of this societal issue, we have to consider the question: how did these rapists become rapists?

Background of an Undetected Rapist

Research has shown that undetected rapists have a history of abuse. As children, these "would be future rapists" were physically abused and could not protect themselves against the adults that controlled, manipulated, and exerted their power of authority and force over their lives (Lisak, 2002). An abused child is powerless to stop their abuser's pursuit for humiliation and assault. More important, they have no control over the emotional ineptitude and moody episodes displayed by their abusers that would eventually result in abuse. For this reason, many of the undetected rapists have problems displaying or connecting with their own emotions, experiencing empathy and worse, believing that they have violated another's rights and committed a crime. Their intent to sexually coerce and use force if the victim says no are more likely if there are no consequences (Edwards, Bradshaw, and Hinsz 2014). These rapacious behaviors can be matched to the behaviors they would have experienced as victims of abuse in childhood. Additionally, their sexually aggressive behaviors and hostile ideas towards women are long-held beliefs.

Hostile Sexism

Based in hostile sexism, antipathy against women is linked to sexual assault and rape (Taschler and West 2017). One reason is because it reinforces male dominance and power over women. Men view women to be manipulative, deceitful, distrustful, and the cause of their problems (Edwards, Bradshaw and Hinsz 2014). Women are sex objects to be used and discarded. The sexual prejudice against women is directly linked to hostile sexism in which physical violence is often displayed and perpetrated to enhance the rapist's intent to use dominance. They don't trust their victims' words or actions and will blame her for the circumstances of the rape. Most believe that they are not raping their victim but need to use force to complete the act. Additionally, hostile men believe one or all of the rape myths below:

a. lust, pleasure, and passion—she wanted it!
b. the victim's provocative clothing
c. the environment (frat house, house party, etc.)
d. substance usage (drinks or drugs)
e. how late she allowed the predator to stay at her house
f. the victim truly wanted sex because she never said no

These are ideas that help the perpetrators deflect responsibility from their actions and blame their victim (Rape Victim Advocates 2018). Hostile sexism encourages perpetrators to justify their actions and solidify their belief system of rape myths. Their inability to see wrong enhances their masculinity. Most sexually hostile males, have friends that also share the same views, live in environments where other men support their negative beliefs about women, and engage in activities that promote the manipulation and dominance of women (sports activities and fraternities) in order to reinforce their hypermasculinity (Edwards, Bradshaw, and Hinsz 2014). Nowhere are examples of hostile sexism more evident than in the multiple rape accusations of Harvey Weinstein.

Harvey Weinstein

With the Harvey Weinstein scandal that unfolded like a storyline in one of Mr. Weinstein's financed movies, eighty-four women accused the media mogul of sexual misconduct, harassment and assault that spanned over more than twenty years (Moniuszko and Kelly 2017). Academy Award-winning actresses such as Miro Sirvino, Angelina Jolie, Gwyneth Paltrow, Lupita Nyong'o are among the victims of Weinstein's sexual predation (Desta and

Busis 2017). But countless actresses retell nearly identical stories of a rich and powerful man that used his privilege and social capital as a tool to coerce them to take private meetings in his hotel rooms dressed in only a bathrobe, provide him with massages, or force his way into their dressing rooms and hotel rooms demanding lewd sexual acts. Annabella Sciorra recounts how Weinstein forcibly raped her in her home by grabbing her, violently shoving her onto her bed, pinning her to the bed while holding her hands above her head. He ejaculated on her leg and then attempted to perform oral sex (Adams and Otis 2017). Weinstein continued to sexually harass Sciorra for years and across two continents, where he would send cars for her while on location, book hotel rooms next to her room, and bang on her door until she summoned hotel staff to her room for help.

Yet in 2017, she felt ashamed of her actions on the night she was raped in 1992. The guilt associated with the belief that she had done something wrong by opening up her apartment door to him, had completely overwhelmed and almost prevented her from telling her story (Farrow 2017). What's more powerful is that in several of the accounts but not often stated was the complicity of corporate executives, studio heads, attorneys, production assistants, Weinstein's brother, house staff, other actresses, and actors who knew of the stories, sexual exploits, harassment, and rapes, but either covered it up with non-disclosure agreements, gave him money for fines, said nothing, or provided warnings without help. All forms of inaction by the Hollywood community that sheltered Weinstein when they carried the rumors to others but did not report his countless felonies to the authorities can be allied with DIIS theory. He was rewarded, able to keep his job, and amass wealth, while he enhanced his status and power in the community and continued his business as usual. Additionally, it is contributed to offender blameworthiness and the intersectionality of gender, status, and class.

More important is the blinding evidence of complicity at the corporate level regarding the renewal of his 2015 contract which include inaction of accountability consequences. It included clauses that prevented him from being fired as a result of sexual misconduct and assault (Bird and Alexander 2017). It was clear that the Weinstein Company would not pursue criminal charges against Mr. Weinstein when sexual assault allegations were reported in March 2015 (Zeitchik 2015).

Ironically, when the allegations first surfaced, Mr. Weinstein was not immediately fired, it took 63 allegations before the Weinstein Company finally took action in October 2017 (two years after the renewal of his contract). His fall from grace was swift and severe. Like most sexual predators with high recidivism rates, denial and minimization is used as basic defense that is attributed to DIIS theory (Langton, et al. 2008). He was fired from the Weinstein Company and resigned from the board of the company owned by Disney (Barnes 2017). But it took two years for the company to take an aggressive stance. At the time of the writing of this book, Mr. Weinstein was indicted in a New York court as a result of his rampant sexual assault history. Several accusers were pursuing civil cases against Mr. Weinstein and potentially the Weinstein Company for their role in the cover-up of these sexual assaults. He is currently serving a twenty-three-year sentence for one count of third-degree rape and first degree criminal sexual assault (Levenson, del Valle & Moghe, 2020) and his second criminal trial in he was indicted for four counts of rape, and seven sexual assault charges is expected to begin in early 2022 (Puente, 2021). However, his sexual misconduct allegations date back to the 1970s and can be linked to his hypermasculinity.

Hypermasculinity

Males that display the hypermasculine persona possess a need to display and exercise the strength of their prowess with criminal dominance and the sexual violation of their victims Pazzani, 2007; Stander, et al., 2018). Hypermasculinity embodies the ideals that men are strong, anti-feminine, show little to no emotion, and aggressively proud. They are highly competitive and use sports as a way to express their masculinity. Associated with the sex hormone testosterone, hypermasculinity is channeled into sexual pursuits (Michael 2017). Most will have larger than normal sexual appetites and consider women as sexual conquests. A life goal may be to sleep with as many women as possible. As the number of sexual conquests increases, the more it validates hypermasculinity. The use of force becomes part of the sexual conquest, and the rape feeds his sexual appetite beliefs while validating his implicit need to maintain the illusion of virility. Their inability to express more feminine traits such as compassion, empathy, sympathy, and tenderness supports the hypermasculine ideal. However, it also disguises the past pains of vulnerability from childhood. Most rapists have identified strained or broken relationships with their fathers.

While 60 percent of rapists were raised in fatherless homes (Father's Rights 2011), approximately twenty million children in America are being raised in fatherless homes (National Center for Fathering 2018). And for those whose fathers are in the home, their dads are emotionally distant. As a role model for young boys across the country, their father's may exhibit hypermasculine belief systems, where the women is to blame, is often dominated in the household, and relegated to female chores. Modern day traditionalists' households continue to provide this model. But the problem becomes magnified when coupled with physical or sexual abuse of the youth. When the child can't defend themselves against his abuser and no one will help, listen to their pleas or screams, intervene or speak up for them, then warp belief systems are created. If the abuse happens at earlier stages of development (under the age of five), and continues into their teens, they believe that abuse is normal. An abused child may blame their mother when the abuser is a father and as the cycle of abuse increases, the child learns the roles of victim and the methods of domination with aggression and force from the abuser. This *does not* imply that all abused children will become predators, but they will learn the distinct roles of the abuse cycle. Some will disguise their abuse by adopting hypermasculine traits and characteristics. They will befriend other broken children with similar ideals and nurture their own warped beliefs with sexual experiences in which they wield all the power and control. These are the factors that help breed a nation of undetected rapists who can't possibly show compassion and empathy towards their victims or label themselves rapists with criminal intentions. There are more undetected rapists in American society than detected rapists who will not be prosecuted for their criminal activities and will not spend a night in jail if we don't change our actions, perceptions, methods toward sexual assault, and the laws that govern these abuses.

Conclusion

The application of the DIIS theory can be linked to the focal concerns theory in which offender blameworthiness, public safety, social costs, consequences, and prosecution must be considered. Denial, inaction, and information suppression can often be found in various institutions use the belief of consent as a method to avoid a thorough investigation or assign accountability, impose consequences or sanctions, or alert the public regarding undetected rapists and predator offenders. These systematic cover-ups by social and political institutions can lead to the revictimization of survivors that has long lasting effects on their intrapsychic perceptions. The roles that normalized gender scripts, hypersexuality and hypermasculinity play in the sociopathy of an undetected rapist must be further investigated. Although well-known cases of powerful and dominant men like Weinstein, Cosby, and Nassar have shed light on the pervasive rape culture unmasked by the #MeToo movement, the number of undetected and underreported rapists continues to increase. Chapter 6 will examine the methods that provide solutions in order to address the current climate of victim blaming and shaming while considering the public policy amendments and modifications that should be adopted.

CHAPTER SIX

~

A Path Forward, Policy Reform, and Conclusions

Changing Policy: A Slow Process

When allegations of sexual crimes are brought to light against powerful men, non-disclosure agreements prevent accountability and others from learning about the quid pro quo abuses. Social movements like #MeToo are not enough to change policies on the micro and macro level regarding rape and sexual assault (Sabatier and Weible 2014). Policy changes are slow and incremental when moving from the micropolitical to macropolitical arena. But when public opinion shifts with hot button issues and begins to focus on policy failures, government officials begin to take notice of national conversations that begin to institute real policy change. This is best explained by *multiple streams theory* that includes the convergence of three streams (a) problems, (b) politics, and (c) policy (Kingdon 2010). New policies require new solutions that address old problems, and the multiple streams approach identifies a "policy window of opportunity" that opens up to bring forth policy changes. For centuries, sexual violence has permeated every part of society. When applying intersectionality, it is gender problem where the victims are mainly girls and children who are victimized by males from all walks of life (i.e., poor, rich, young, old, powerful, clergy, etc.) (Gravelin, Biernat and Buche 2019). Most know their attacker and are more likely to be shamed, blamed, and judged harshly by others because they know predator (Deblinger, et al. 2010). This is often where the ignorance of America's sexual assault and rape culture begins to expose itself.

Problem

The systematic silencing of victims starts at the local level and continues with reporting. The normalization of hypermasculinity, hostile sexism, and hyper-sexuality of American males creates environments of dominance and control where females are most vulnerable and traditional ritualistic practice governs gender scripts (Gravelin, Biernat, and Buche 2019). Once an assault occurs, responses and lines of questioning from trusted family and friends, hospital staff, and law enforcement, if not supportive, can re-traumatize a victim and exacerbate mental health issues (Classen, et al. 2005; Finkelhor, Ormrod, & Turner, 2007; Papalia, et al, 2017; RAINN, 2019). Discrediting victims that are under the influence of substances during the sexual assault and errone-ously defining this a "false claims" or as consent limits disclosure and leads to a nationwide backlog of untested rape kits or the destruction of these kits by law enforcement agencies (End the Backlog 2019). Prosecutors may be culpable for the low prosecution rates of sex crimes when they decide not to prosecute an assailant because the victim can be easily discredited because of previously mentioned factors. To date, five cases out of one thousand cases receive convictions (Loofbourow 2019). Increased prosecutions may serve as a deterrent to sexual predators. But there is an opportunity for policy change.

Policy Solutions

When addressing solutions that target sexual assault and rape against chil-dren and teens, federal grooming laws were established when sex offenders target minors. This federal statute titled Coercion and Enticement § 2422 Title 18 USCS (b) addresses traveling interstate, engaging in sexual activ-ity with minors, prostitution, trafficking or using the mail system to entice and coerce a child under the age of eighteen will receive a sentence of ap-proximately twenty years (Pollack 2015). Several states have adopted similar statutes. In order to address the sexual predation of minors, parents must be trained on the importance of grooming. Additionally, children must be trained to identify adult grooming. Parents may believe that children are too young to learn about grooming, but elementary school children as young as five years old must learn about adults that use grooming techniques (School Counseling By Heart 2012). This is not a case of "stranger danger," groom-ing is perpetrated by a known, and trusted family member or ally. Prevention tactics must begin at earlier stages of development and should not be littered with fear, shame, and anxiety (Pollack 2015). The statistics don't lie about child sexual abuse—"every nine minutes a child abuse claim is substantiated" (RAINN 2018). But Coercion and Enticement § 2422 Title 18 USCS (a) addresses minors under eighteen years old targeted by grooming. Prevention tactics at every age and grade can be great policy solutions. Remember, eighty-two of victims of sexual assault are under the age of eighteen and are female (Finkelhor, Shattuck, et al., 2014). Reporting must be encouraged and websites like Right2Consent.com, assist victims with their report. It presents the questions that most first responders will ask, and once completed, provides a print out that can be sent to a supportive friend's email and taken to the police interview (Right 2 Consent 2021).

Law Enforcement and Survivors of Sexual Assault

Nationwide law enforcement agencies must be held accountable for their negligence when working with sex assault and rape reporting (Campbell & Raja, 1999; Campbell & Ferhler-Cabral, 2018). As first responders, victim centered training must be state mandated. Judgment, blame, and shame should not be tactics used in the interview process after a sex assault. The Office of Justice Programs provides continuing education units from the Office for Victims of Crime Training & Technical Assistance Center (OVC TTAC). This training addresses the importance of DNA collection and testing and sex assault training for nurses, advocates, and law enforcement (Office of Justice Program 2020). Victims have often expressed disappointment with the way they are treated by first responders (Monahan and Polk 2020). These interactions are expected to provide support and empathy for victims. However, interviews from first responders can be seen as interrogations that may re-traumatize and cast doubt about credible claims of harm (Campbell and Raja, 1999; Campbell & Ferhler-Cabral, 2018). First responders (i.e., police officers) hold cultural bias that includes gender scripts and bias. If mandatory rape kit submission within five to ten days is required of all law enforcement agencies, evidence can be gathered and the backlog can decrease (End the Backlog 2019). Additionally, prosecutors may have the evidence needed for criminal indictments. Prosecutors and defense attorneys must also be held accountable for their limiting beliefs and bias that have negatively judged the credibility of victims and decisions not to prosecute an offender (Yarbough 2021). This has repeatedly served as a deterrent for disclosure reporting (Monahan and Polk 2020). Bystander training has successfully helped reduce sexual assault on university and colleges campuses (Moynihan and Banyard 2008). This can be a mandatory training provided by residence life and campus activity boards with assigned roles that help combat gender scripts. When members of the campus community are assigned proactive roles that help reduce victimization of vulnerable people at campus events, it helps raise awareness and change social norms (National Sexual Violence Resource Center 2013). Individual responsibility for victimization gets shifted to the community's responsibility of safety—keeping members of the community safe. With focal concerns theory, two elements can be applied to offender blameworthiness and keeping the public safe. Several bystanders can be assigned to the role of safety monitoring of vulnerable attendees. Bystanders can become witnesses in the event a sex assault occurs at the campus event. These mandatory trainings can be required of all campus groups (i.e., fraternities, sororities, athletic groups, etc.). Last, rehabilitation for sex offenders should be considered in order to reduce the number of repeat offenders and recidivism. At some point, sex offenders will be released from jail and return to local communities. Can these offenders be redeemed after they have served their time, and should they be able to return to their careers? Tarana Burke believes redemption is possible and rehabilitation that helps offenders "make dramatic shifts in their behavior" is essential (Smith 2019). Various forms of programs were developed to target repetitive psychological thought loops and behaviors that facilitated hypersexual, hostile sexism, and hypermasculine ideologies (National Institute of Justice 2020). Counseling programs such as cognitive behavioral therapy in a group setting can address the thoughts and behaviors that create the deviancy. Psychotherapy can be used to explore past experiences that may expose some of the underlying causes of the use sexual violence. Medical castration is another option that uses hormonal therapy to reduce the amount of testosterone produced and inhibit an erection. Some men have opted for this solution combined with psychotherapy and it is completely voluntary (Tsoulis-Reay 2015). Several states (Alabama, California, Louisiana, Florida, and Wisconsin) have passed laws to institute medical/chemical castration to reduce recidivism of sex offenders (Blinder 2019). But these methodologies are expected to address "accountability and assumption of responsibility that sex offenders often avoid (Hubbard 2014). These solutions instituted on the macropolitical level and enforced at the micropolitical may begin to shift the zeitgeist from past decades and centuries of gender disparity in sexual assault and rape cases to create a policy window that policy entrepreneurs can use to their advantage.

Politics

With the #MeToo movement demanding that public opinion change from victim blame and shame to "believe me," politicians have begun to use their bully pulpit to set agendas and create bills that denounce America's rape culture and address reporting. For example, Senator Joni Ernst addressed statutes thus allowing extensions for reporting. She has also proposed several bills that address sexual assault in the military, college campuses and the reporting of sexual assault with U.S. athletic organizations (Joni Ernst United States Senator for Iowa n.d.). Additionally, Kirsten Gillibrand, with bipartisan support created the Military Justice Improvement Act to support military personnel who are sexually harassed and assaulted (Gillibrand 2019). There is a mandate in the act to make sexual harassment a crime, but the problem is—will the Act get adopted? It must past the sixty vote filibuster in which a majority of votes (forty-one plus votes) may knock out bills from proposal. Policymakers are not able to address every cause, bill or solution proposed by lobbyists and are often faced with time constraints and deadlines to propose a bill for consideration (Sabatier and Weible 2014). For this reason, statewide ballot initiatives can provide a solution.

States can introduce sexual assault related initiatives for enactment and enforcement with the help of ballot initiatives. *Ballot initiatives* can be sponsored by various organizations and/or corporations throughout the state that collects the appropriate number of signatures from the public needed to place an initiative on the ballot. States like Arizona, Maine, and Pennsylvania have proposed ballot initiatives that let the public decide if an initiative should become law and by-pass legislative referendums (Ballotpedia, 2017–2021). These initiatives become amendments to the State constitution (Gross 2019). Initiatives can provide solutions to many of the problems that can't be solved with macropolitics. But when these bills are posed to (a) state legislature bodies, (b) lobbying members of the legislature in order set an agenda, (c) to create a bill and obtain votes, these processes can often take years. Additionally, the process can kill a bill if it does not receive a majority vote or is an unpopular partisan initiative (Sabatier and Weible 2014). Sexual assault and rape policies need solutions that equally affect social change on both the micro/macropolitical levels.

~

Conclusion

The goal of this book was to illuminate the need for sociopolitical change that combats the current rape culture in America while explaining the factors associated with victim blame. The pervasive and increasing rates of sexual assault and sexual violence that shames the victim, silences their cries for help with blame and judgment, reduces offender blameworthiness and prosecutes few perpetrators must end. With the underreporting of approximately seventy-five percent of sex crimes, undetected rapists are free to engage in future sexual violence without accountability or prosecution (RAINN, 2019; Lisak & Miller, 2002; Lisak, 2006; Valentine, et al., 2016; Campbell & Fehler-Cabral, 2018). There are various typologies of sexual offenders and there is a distinction between adult and juvenile assailants.

Adult sex offenders may be labeled regressed (female victims) or fixated (male victims) and have specific selection preferences (Mercado, Tallon, and Terry 2008). But some scholars argue that genetics may pay a role in predation. Scandals associated the Catholic Priests and Boys Scouts of America have raised public awareness of the magnitude of sexual assaults against children. However, with approximately forty percent of sexual violence committed by juveniles (Przybylski and Lobanov-Rostovsky 2020), that were once victims, re-victimization in the future is also an issue. A child that is a victim of childhood sexual abuse is likely to experience re-victimization as a result of risky sexual behavioral responses, inability to set sexual boundaries, and the propensity to victimize others (Finkelhor, Ormrod, & Turner, 2007; Finkelhor, Shattuck, et al., 2014). It is likely that Americans may be raising a legion of undetected sex offenders because significant deterrence measures are not repeatedly imposed (Lisak & Miller, 2002).

Schools (K-12, colleges, and universities) are hot spots for sexual assault and with the ever-changing government regulation of Title IX, creating safe school environments that are free of sexual discrimination has become a societal challenge. Denial, inaction, and information suppression (DIIS) of social institutions such as school, churches, organizations, and corporations are the tools used to thwart thorough investigations. Intersectionality of class, prestige, gender, age, race, ethnicity, and disability can be attributed to the negligence of social institutions use of non-disclosure agreements and inability to conduct investigations while blaming the victims or disenfranchised groups. It is not uncommon that these institutions use victim blaming as a defense to silence victims and impede future reporting of sexual violence (Yarbough 2021). Non-disclosure or confidentiality agreements are the weapon of choice used when victims discuss the details of their sexual assault and survivors can be liable and threatened with lawsuits. Well-known cases of prominent figures and celebrities such as Cosby, Weinstein, and Nassar have used NDAs to silence their survivors (Levenson & Cooper, 2018; Connors, 2018; Levenson, del Valle & Moghe, 2020). But when faced with an increasing number of sexual assaults, law enforcements focal concerns of (a) offender blameworthiness, (b) protecting the public, and (c) social costs of the prosecution of the guilty offender, often support the institutions needs at great expense to the victim and/or survivor (Campbell & Fehler-Cabral, 2018).

Davis (1989, p. 49–51) explains that the complete "obliteration" of the epidemic of sexual violence must be "forged on all its myriad of fronts." The normalization of sexual violence against any of America's populace is a black eye against public safety and law enforcement ability to protect and serve. But the fact that the most vulnerable population subjected to sexual violence are teens and children in one of the greatest industrialized nations, is abominable and grotesque. Radical social transformation is obligatory, if the harrowing statistics associated with sexual assault and rape are expected to decline. Kingdon (2010) proposed three streams (a) problems, (b) politics, and (c) policy that can influence the positive outcomes for radical social change efforts. This can include the consistent investigation and use of law enforcement practices that indict, prosecute and sentence offenders.

Criminal justice reform should begin with the requirement to test all sexual assault kits in order to obtain DNA evidence of assailants for potential prosecution (End the Backlog, 2019). Mandatory empathy and compassion training must be provided to all law enforcement, first responders, healthcare providers, campus counselors, teachers, human resource managers, and other significant allies that interact with sexual assault victims and survivors (Office of Justice Program 2020). This can help reduce victim blaming and encourage vulnerable survivors to report the sex crime (Monahan & Polk, 2020). When reporting increases, public awareness increases, and offenders can be held accountable for their actions. Children and teens must learn about grooming tactics from trusted family members, friends, and acquaintances so that they become active participants in reducing sexual victimization. If they are the most vulnerable targets, they must be educated on prevention techniques at earlier stages of development. Empowering the youth with bystander trainings in schools (primary, secondary, and post-secondary) will help re-shape the ways youth view sexual assault and rape. Hypersexual, hypermasculine, and hostile sexism should no longer be normalized as acceptable rape myths and sexual violence acceptance. Last, local, state, and federal public policies should extend statute of limitations for sex crimes, provide mandatory sentencing guidelines, and punitive measures that include rehabilitation for juvenile and adult sex offenders.

~

References

A Better Childhood (January 2, 2020). *A Better Childhood*. Retrieved September 8, 2020, from It's Never Too Late to Have a Better Childhood: http://www.abetter childhood.org/.

A Better Childhood (January 4, 2020). *History: Why We are Here*. Retrieved September 7, 2020, from A Better Childhood: http://www.abetterchildhood.org /history/.

Abrams, R., & Kantor, J. (October 17, 2017). *Gwyneth Paltrow, Angelina Jolie and Others Say Weinstein Harassed Them*. Retrieved January 4, 2020, from The New York Times: https://www.nytimes.com/2017/10/10/us/gwyneth-paltrow-angelina -jolie-harvey-weinstein.html.

Adams Otis, G. (October 27, 2017). *Actress Annabella Sciorra says Harvey Weinstein raped her in her apartment in the '90s*. Retrieved January 15, 2018, from Daily News: Entertainment: http://www.nydailynews.com/entertainment/annabella-sciorra -weinstein-busted-home-raped-article-1.3594479.

Adams, C. (1994). Mothers Who Fail to Protect Their Children from Sexual Abuse: Addressing the Problem of Denial. *Yale Law & Policy Review, 2*, 519–39.

Ali, Y. (November 4, 2017). *Despite 'Overwhelming' Evidence Against Actor Danny Masterson, Rape Case Has Stalled*. Retrieved July 10, 2018, from Huffington Post: https://www.huffingtonpost.com/entry/danny-masterson-rape-accusations _us_59fa8410e4b01b474048242a.

Allen, S. (June 9, 2015). *Marital Rape Is Semi-Legal in 8 States*. Retrieved November 11, 2017, from The Daily Beast: https://www.thedailybeast.com/marital-rape-is -semi-legal-in-8-states.

Almukhtar, S., Gold, M., & Buchanan, L. (February 8, 2018). *After Weinstein: 71 Men Accused of Sexual Misconduct and Their Fall From Power*. Retrieved June 6, 2018, from The New York Times: https://www.nytimes.com/interactive/2017/11/10/us/men-accused-sexual-misconduct-weinstein.html.

American Psychiatric Association (January 1, 2017). *What Is Posttraumatic Stress Disorder?* Retrieved January 2, 2020, from American Psychiatric Association: https://www.psychiatry.org/patients-families/ptsd/what-is-ptsd.

Arizona Coalition To End Sexual and Domestic Violence (January, 2020). *Sexual Violence Myths & Misconceptions: Myth or Fact.* Retrieved January 11, 2020, from Arizona Coalition To End Sexual and Domestic Violence: https://www.acesdv.org/about-sexual-domestic-violence/sexual-violence-myths-misconceptions/.

Arkin, D. (November 25, 2019). *Bill Cosby says he doesn't expect to express remorse after prison sentence.* Retrieved January 19, 2020, from NBC News: https://www.nbcnews.com/news/us-news/bill-cosby-says-he-doesn-t-expect-express-remorse-after-n1090641.

Associated Press (May 20, 2016). *Lawyer: Hugh Hefner gives testimony in Bill Cosby sex case.* Retrieved January 23, 2018, from Associated Press: https://apnews.com/cb2dde99d07541e69a637a3b0f025745/lawyer-hugh-hefner-gives-testimony-bill-cosby-sex-case.

Associated Press (December 11, 2018). *No jail time for ex-Baylor fraternity president accused of rape* . Retrieved December 20, 2019, from Los Angeles Times: https://www.latimes.com/nation/la-na-baylor-frat-rape-accusation-20181211-story.html.

Associated Press (December 18, 2018). *Judge, prosecutors who allowed ex-Baylor fraternity president accused of rape to avoid prison time all have ties to school.* Retrieved December 20, 2019, from Daily News: https://www.nydailynews.com/news/crime/ny-news-baylor-rape-case-ties-school-20181216-story.html.

Associated Press (September 15, 2021). *Olympic gymnasts give emotional testimony to Congress about sexual abuse.* Retrieved from Tampa Bay Times: https://www.tampabay.com/sports/2021/09/15/olympic-gymnasts-give-emotional-testimony-to-congress-about-sexual-abuse/.

Atkinson, T. G. (2014). The Descent from Radical Feminism to Postmodernism. A *Revolutionary Moment: Women's Liberation in the Late 1960s and the Early 1970s* (pp. 1–4). Boston: Boston University.

Augustine, K. (May 13, 2019). *The difference between 'victim' and 'survivor'.* Retrieved from The Daily Northwestern: https://dailynorthwestern.com/2019/05/13/lateststories/augustine-the-difference-between-victim-and-survivor/.

Ballotpedia (February 1, 2017). *Arizona Judges Allowed to Decline Bail for Certain Crimes, Proposition 103 (2002).* Retrieved April 15, 2021, from Ballotpedia: https://ballotpedia.org/Arizona_Judges_Allowed_to_Decline_Bail_for_Certain_Crimes,_Proposition_103_(2002).

Ballotpedia (November 1, 2020). *Maine Minimum Sentences for Sexual Assault Against Children Under Age 12 Initiative (2020).* Retrieved April 15, 2021, from Ballotpedia: https://ballotpedia.org/Maine_Minimum_Sentences_for_Sexual_Assault_Against_Children_Under_Age_12_Initiative_(2020).

Ballotpedia (January 1, 2021). *Pennsylvania Childhood Sexual Abuse Retroactive Lawsuits for Two-Year Period Amendment (2021)*. Retrieved April 15, 2021, from Ballotpedia: https://ballotpedia.org/Pennsylvania_Childhood_Sexual_Abuse _Retroactive_Lawsuits_for_Two-Year_Period_Amendment_(2021).

Banvard-Fox, C., Linger, M., Paulson, D. J., Cottrell, L., & Davidov, D. M. (June, 2020). Sexual Assault in Adolescents. *Primary Care: Clinics in Office Practice, 47*(2), 331–49.

Bardaglio, P. W. (November, 1994). Rape and the Law in the Old South: "Calculated to Excite Indignation in Every Heart. *The Journal of Southern History, 60*(4), 749-72.

Barnes, B. (October 17, 2017). *Harvey Weinstein, Fired on Oct. 8, Resigns From Company's Board*. Retrieved January 8, 2018, from The NY Times: https://www.ny times.com/2017/10/17/business/media/harvey-weinstein-sexual-harassment.html.

Barnett, M. D., Sligar, K. B., & Wang, C. D. (2018). Religiosity, Gender, and Rape Myth Acceptance: Feminist Theory and Rape Culture. *Journal of Interpersonal Violence, 33*(8), 1219–1235.

Basile, K. C., Chen, J. B., & Saltzman, L. E. (2007). Basile, K. C., Chen, J., Black, M. C., Saltzman, L. E. . *Violence and Victims, 22*, 437–38.

Basu, T. (July 28, 2015). *Donald Trump Lawyer Sorry for Saying 'You Can't Rape Your Spouse'*. Retrieved November 18, 2017, from Time: http://time.com/3974560 /donald-trump-rape-ivana-michael-cohen/.

Bauer-Wolf, J. (October 21, 2019). *Civil liberties watchdog FIRE debuts due process, Title IX tracker*. Retrieved January 4, 2020, from Education Dive: https://www .educationdive.com/news/due-process-database-premieres/565504/.

BBC (January 31, 2018). *Larry Nassar case: USA Gymnastics doctor 'abused 265 girls'*. Retrieved March 24, 2018, from BBC: http://www.bbc.com/news/world-us -canada-42894833.

Bernsten, L. (March 21, 2017). *The Science of Victim Blaming*. Retrieved November 30, 2019, from Huffington Post: https://www.huffpost.com/entry/the-science-of -victim-blaming_b_58d07585e4b07112b647311a.

Bhuptani, P., & Messman, T. L. (2021). Role of blame and rape-related shame in distress among rape victims. *Psychological Trauma: Theory, Research, Practice, and Policy*, 52–61.

Bible Gateway (n.d.). *2 Samuel 13*. Retrieved November 29, 2017, from Bible Gateway: https://www.biblegateway.com/passage/?search=2+Samuel+13.

Bible Gateway (n.d.). *Genesis 34: Dinah and the Shechemites*. Retrieved November 29, 2017, from Bible Gateway: https://www.biblegateway.com/passage/?search=Genesis 34.

Bible Gateway (n.d.). *Judges 19-21*. Retrieved November 29, 2017, from Bible Gateway: https://www.biblegateway.com/passage/?search=Judges+19-21&version =NABRE

Biography (August 28, 2018). *Recy Taylor Biography*. Retrieved December 15, 2019, from Biography: https://www.biography.com/activist/recy-taylor.

Bird, S., & Alexander, H. (October 13, 2017). *Harvey Weinstein's contract 'protected him from sexual harassment allegations*. Retrieved January 8, 2018, from The Telegraph: http://www.telegraph.co.uk/news/2017/10/13/harvey-weinsteins-contract -protected-sexual-harassment-allegations/.

Bishop, K. (April 15, 2018). *A Reflection on the History of Sexual Assault Laws in the United States*. Retrieved November 30, 2019, from The Arkansas Journal of Social Change and Public Service: https://ualr.edu/socialchange/2018/04/15/reflection -history-sexual-assault-laws-united-states/.

Blinder, A. (June 11, 2019). *What to Know About the Alabama Chemical Castration Law*. Retrieved January 10, 2020, from The New York Times: https://www.ny times.com/2019/06/11/us/politics/chemical-castration.html.

Blistein, J. (December 13, 2021). *USA Gymnastics, the U.S. Olympic and Paralympic Committee*. Retrieved from Rolling Stone: https://www.rollingstone.com/culture /culture-news/larry-nassar-abuse-survivors-settlement-usa-gymnastics-olympics -1270890/.

Block, S., & Culture, O. I. (2006). *Rape and Sexual Power in Early America*. Williamsburg, Virginia, U.S.A.: Chapel Hill: Omohundro Institute and University of North Carolina Press.

Blumer, H. (November 10, 1971). Social Problems As Collective Behavior. *Social Problems, 18*(3), 298–306.

Boardman, M. (July 29, 2015). *My Husband Raped Me*. Retrieved November 11, 2017, from Time: http://time.com/3976180/marital-rape/.

Boyle, K. M., & Walker, L. S. (December, 2016). The Neutralization and Denial of Sexual Violence in College Party Subcultures. *Deviant Behavior, 37*(12), 1392–410.

Broman-Fulks, J. J., Ruggiero, K. J., Hanson, R. F., Smith, D. W., Resnick, H. S., Kilpatrick, D. G., & Saunders, B. E. (April 1, 2007). BRIEF REPORT: Sexual Assault Disclosure in Relation to Adolescent Mental Health: Results from the National Survey of Adolescents. *Journal of Clinical Child & Adolescent Psychology, 36*(2), 260–66.

Brown, A., Kouri, N., & Hirst, W. (2012). Memory's malleability: its role in shaping collective memory and social identity. *Frontiers in Psychology*.

Buchbinder, E., & Sinay, D. (2020). Incest Survivors' Life-Narratives. Violence Against Women, 26(8), 803–24.

Burgess, L. (March 30, 2018). *This Is What PTSD Looks Like for Sexual Assault Survivors*. Retrieved January 2, 2020, from Brit & Co: https://www.brit.co/what-ptsd -looks-like-for-sexual-assault-survivors/.

California Coalition Against Sexual Assault. (March, 2017). *SAAM Ending sexual violence: An intersectional approach*. Retrieved April 12, 2021, from CALCASA: https://www.calcasa.org/wp-content/uploads/2017/03/SAAM-2017-reduced-size -edited.pdf.

Cambridge Dictionary. (2021). *Meaning of diss*. Retrieved from Cambridge Dictionary: https://dictionary.cambridge.org/dictionary/english/diss

Campbell, R., & Fehler-Cabral, G. (March, 2018). Why police "couldn't or wouldn't" submit sexual assault kits for forensic dna testing: a focal concerns theory analysis of untested rape kits. *Law & Society Review, 52*(1), 73–105.

Campbell, R., & Raja, S. (October, 1999). Secondary Victimization of Rape Victims. *Violence and Victims, 14*(3), 261–75.

Campbell, R., Brown Sprague, H., Cottrill, S., & Sullivan, C. (2011). Longitudinal research with sexual assault survivors: a methodological review. *Journal of Interpersonal Violence, 26*(3), 433–61.

Campbell, R., Greeson, M. R., Fehler-Cabral, G., & Kennedy, A. (2015). Pathways to help: Adolescent sexual assault victims' disclosure and help-seeking experiences. *Violence Against Women, 21*(7), 824–47.

Campbell, R., Patterson, D., Bybee, D., & Dworkin, E. R. (2009). Predicting sexual assault prosecution outcomes: The role of medical forensic evidence collected by sexual assault nurse examiners. *Criminal Justice and Behavior, 36*, 712–27.

Campbell, R., Pierce, S. J., Sharma, D. B., Feeney, H., & Fehler, C. G. (2016). Should rape kit testing be prioritized by victim-offender relationship? *Criminology & Public Policy, 15*(2), 555–83.

Cassada Lohmann, R., & Raja, S. (2016). *The Sexual Trauma Workbook for Teen Girls: A Guide to Recovery From Sexual Assault and Abuse*. Oakland, CA, U.S.A.: New Harbinger Publications, Inc.

Chen, J. (June 22, 2017). *Bill Cosby Sexual Assault Mistrial: Two Jurors Prevented Guilty Verdict*. Retrieved March 24, 2018, from Rolling Stone: https://www.rollingstone.com/culture/news/bill-cosby-mistrial-two-jurors-prevented-guilty-verdict-w489198

Choudhary, E., Smith, M., & Bossarte, R. (January 1, 2012). Depression, anxiety, and symptom profiles among female and male victims of sexual violence. *American Journal of Men's Health, 6*(1), 28–36.

Christensen, K. (May 15, 2019). *Boy Scout sex abuse scandal's stunning toll: Over 12,200 reported victims*. Retrieved November 23, 2019, from Los Angeles Times: https://www.latimes.com/local/california/la-na-boy-scouts-child-sex-abuse-2019 0515-story.html.

Christensen, M., & Harris, R. (December, 2019). Correlates of bystander readiness to help among a diverse college student population: an intersectional perspective. *Research in Higher Education, 60*(8), 1195–1226.

Clarke, S. (January 4, 2018). *Anthony Rapp Opens Up About Kevin Spacey Allegations, Says Culture of Abuse Is 'Being Dismantled'*. Retrieved January 4, 2020, from Variety: https://variety.com/2018/film/news/anthony-rapp-kevin-spacey-sexual-misconduct-abuse-culture-1202653164/.

Classen, C. C., Palesh, O. G., & Aggarwal, R. (2005). Sexual revictimization: A review of the empirical literature. *Trauma, Violence, & Abuse, 6*(2), 103–29.

Clayton, E., Jones, C., Brown, J., & Taylor, J. (May, 2018). The aetiology of child sexual abuse: a critical review of the empirical evidence. *Child Abuse Review, 27*(3), 181–197.

Conaboy, K. (December 1, 2016). *Familiarize Yourself With Casey Affleck's Sexual Harassment Allegations*. Retrieved June 7, 2018, from The Hairpin: https://www .thehairpin.com/2016/12/familiarize-yourself-with-casey-afflecks-sexual-harass ment-allegations/#.2hp1ee6qg.

Connors, R. (February 18, 2018). *Michigan State*. Retrieved June 4, 2018, from Larry Nassar case: What you need to know about former Michigan State, USA Gymnas- tics doctor: https://www.landof10.com/michigan-state/larry-nassar-case-michigan -state-sexual-assault.

Conti, A. (June , 2016). *A Brief and Depressing History of Rape Laws*. Retrieved December 7, 2019, from Vice.com: https://www.vice.com/en_us/article/9bkje5/for -context-heres-how-various-societies-punished-rapists.

Cornwell, S. (December 13, 2018). *Congress passes bill to make members pay sexual misconduct claims*. Retrieved December 20, 2019, from Reuters: https://www .reuters.com/article/us-usa-congress-harassment/congress-passes-bill-to-make -members-pay-sexual-misconduct-claims-idUSKBN1OC2V0.

Coulter, R. W., & Rankin, S. R. (March 15, 2017). College Sexual Assault and Campus Climate for Sexual- and Gender-Minority Undergraduate Students. *Jour- nal of Interpersonal Violence, 35*(5–6), 1351–66.

Counts, J. (June 5, 2018). *Ex-dean William Strampel had MSU-themed pornography on computer, officials testify*. Retrieved June 5, 2018, from Michigan News: http:// www.mlive.com/news/index.ssf/2018/06/william_strampel_had_msu-theme.html.

Coxell, A. E., & King, M. B. (November 10, 2010). Male victims of rape and sexual abuse. *Sexual & Relationship Therapy, 25*(4), 380–91.

Culp-Ressler, T. (May 14, 2014). *Columbia Students Are Writing The Names Of Accused Rapists On Bathroom Walls*. Retrieved January 30, 2020, from Think Progress: https://thinkprogress.org/columbia-students-are-writing-the-names-of -accused-rapists-on-bathroom-walls-a948e499c5c/.

Darkness to Light. (n.d.). *Child Sexual Abuse Statistics*. Retrieved November 17, 2017, from Darkness to Light: End Sexual Abuse: https://www.d2l.org/the-issue /statistics/

Darrah, N. (January 31, 2018). *Fox News*. Retrieved March 24, 2018, from Michi- gan cops to apologize for believing Larry Nassar over 17-year-old victim: http:// www.foxnews.com/us/2018/01/31/michigan-cops-to-apologize-for-believing-larry -nassar-over-17-year-old-victim.html.

Davis, A. (2021). Resolving the tension between feminism and evolutionary psy- chology: An epistemological critique. *Evolutionary Behavioral Sciences*, 368–88.

Deblinger, E., Thakkar-Kolar, R., Berry, E., & Schroeder, C. (2010). Caregivers' ef- forts to educate their children about child sexual abuse. *Child Maltreatment, 15*(1), 91–100.

DeCou, C. R., Cole, T. T., Lynch, S. M., Wong, M. M., & Matthews, K. C. (March 1, 2017). Assault-Related Shame Mediates the Association Between Negative Social Reactions to Disclosure of Sexual Assault and Psychological Distress. *Psy- chological Trauma: Theory, Research, Practice, and Policy, 9*(2), 166–72.

Desta, Y., & Busis, H. (October 12, 2017). *These are the women who have accused Harvey Weinstein of Sexual Harassment and Assault.* Retrieved January 15, 2018, from Vanity Fair: Hollywood: https://www.vanityfair.com/hollywood/2017/10/harvey-weinstein-accusers-sexual-harassment-assault-rose-mcgowan-ashley-judd-gwyneth-paltrow.

Dockterman, E. (January 25, 2017). *What to Know About the Casey Affleck Oscar Controversy.* Retrieved July 3, 2018, from Time: http://time.com/4645846/what-to-know-about-the-casey-affleck-oscar-controversy/.

Dockterman, E. (June 1, 2019). *These Men Say the Boy Scouts' Sex Abuse Problem Is Worse Than Anyone Knew* . Retrieved October 8, 2020, from Time: https://time.com/longform/boy-scouts-sex-abuse/.

Donovan, P. (2016). A *"New" Problem Appears in the 1990s: The Birth of the Contemporary Date Rape Drugs Scare. In: Drink Spiking and Predatory Drugging.* New York, NY, USA: Palgrave Macmillan.

Donovan, P. (2016). A *"New" Problem Appears in the 1990s: The Birth of the Contemporary Date Rape Drugs Scare. In: Drink Spiking and Predatory Drugging.* New York, NY, USA: Palgrave Macmillan.

Du Mont, J., Miller, K.-L., & Myhr, T. L. (April, 2003). The Role of "Real Rape" and "Real Victim" Stereotypes in the Police Reporting Practices of Sexually Assaulted Women. *Violence Against Women* , 9(4), 466–86.

Ducharme, J. (March 7, 2019). *'Don't Let Your Assaulter Rob You of Your Future':* Sen. Martha McSally Revealed Her Rape to Empower Survivors. Retrieved January 3, 2020, from Time: https://time.com/5546945/martha-mcsally-cbs-interview/

Dunne, E. A. (2011). Clerical child sex abuse: the response of the roman catholic church. *Journal of Community & Applied Social Psychology, 14*(6), 490–94.

Eagle, G., & Kaminer, D. (2013). Continuous traumatic stress: Expanding the lexicon of traumatic stress. *Peace and Conflict: Journal of Peace Psychology, 19*(2), 85–99.

Edwards, S. R. (December 15, 2014). Denying rape but endorsing forceful intercourse: Exploring differences among responders. *Violence and Gender, 1*(4), 188–93.

Eisenberg, M. E., Lust, K., Mathiason, A., M., & Porta, C. M. (August 21, 2017). Sexual assault, sexual orientation, and reporting among college students. *Journal of Interpersonal Violence.*

Elber, L. (January 18, 2018). *Rose McGowan forced to sell house to pay for legal battle with Harvey Weinstein.* Retrieved January 3, 2020, from Global News: https://globalnews.ca/news/3955582/rose-mcgowan-sell-her-home-to-pay-for-legal-battle-harvey-weinstein/.

Elber, L. (January 18, 2018). *Rose McGowan forced to sell house to pay for legal battle with Harvey Weinstein.* Retrieved January 3, 2020, from Global News: https://globalnews.ca/news/3955582/rose-mcgowan-sell-her-home-to-pay-for-legal-battle-harvey-weinstein/.

Ence, J. (2019). I like you when you are silent": the future of NDAs and mandatory arbitration in the era of #metoo. *Journal of Dispute Resolution, 2019*(2), 165–79.

End the Backlog (March 8, 2019). *What is the Rape Kit Backlog?* Retrieved January 4, 2020, from End the Backlog: http://www.endthebacklog.org/backlog/what-rape-kit-backlog.

End The Backlog (November 29, 2019). *Where the Backlog Exists and What's Happening to End It* (J. H. Foundation, Producer). Retrieved December 28, 2010, from End the Backlog: http://www.endthebacklog.org/backlog/why-backlog-exists.

Engel, P. (June 5, 2017). *Bill Cosby's sexual-assault trial starts today—here's the backstory of the allegations against him.* Retrieved January 18, 2018, from Business Insider: http://www.businessinsider.com/andrea-constand-bill-cosby-trial-2017-6.

Estrich, S. (1988). *Real Rape.* Cambridge, MA: Harvard University Press.

Fargo, J. D. (2009). Pathways to Adult Sexual Revictimization: Direct and Indirect Behavioral Risk Factors Across the Lifespan. *Journal of Interpersonal Violence,* 24(11), 1771–91.

Farrow, R. (October 27, 2017). *Weighing the Costs of Speaking Out About Harvey Weinstein Annabella Sciorra, Daryl Hannah, and other women explain their struggles with going public.* Retrieved January 15, 2018, from The New Yorker: https://www.newyorker.com/news/news-desk/weighing-the-costs-of-speaking-out-about-harvey-weinstein.

Father's Rights. (March 2, 2011). *The Effects of Father Absence on Children.* Retrieved June 11, 2018, from Father's Rights: http://dadsrights.com/wp-content/uploads/2011/03/fatherabsence.pdf.

Federal Bureau of Investigation Criminal Justice Information Services Division. (2013). *Rape Addendum.* Washington, D.C., USA: U.S. Department of Justice.

Federal Bureau of Investigations. (2014). *Frequently Asked Questions about the Change in the UCR Definition of Rape.* Washington, D.C., USA: Federal Bureau of Investigations.

Federal Bureau of Investigations. (2017). *2016 Crime statistics released: Violent crime increase, property crime decreases.* Washington, D.C., USA: Federal Bureau of Investigations.

Felson, R. B., & Palmore, C. (2018). Biases in blaming victims of rape and other crime. *Psychology of Violence,* 390–99.

Fields, A. (October 28, 2016). *UW students publish online 'rape list' out of hopelessness.* Retrieved January 30, 2020, from The Seattle Times: https://www.seattletimes.com/seattle-news/education/uw-students-publish-online-rape-list-out-of-hopelessness-community-reels/.

Finkelhor, D. (1984). *Child sexual abuse : new theory and research.* New York, NY, United States of America: Free Press.

Finkelhor, D. (1994). The international epidemiology of child sexual abuse. *Child Abuse & Neglect,* 18, 409–17.

Finkelhor, D., & Araji, S. (1986). Explanations of pedophilia: A four factor model. *The Journal of Sex Research,* 22(2), 145–61.

Finkelhor, D., Ormrod, R., & Turner, H. (2007). Re-victimization patterns in a national longitudinal sample of children and youth. *Child Abuse & Neglect, 31,* 479–502.

Finkelhor, D., Shattuck, A., Turner, H., & Hamby, S. L. (September, 2014). *Journal of Adolescent Health, 55*(3), 329–33.

Fishel, J. (November 17, 2017). *Congress secretly paid nearly $100,000 to settle harassment claims against disgraced congressman.* Retrieved December 18, 2019, from ABC News: https://abcnews.go.com/Politics/congress-secretly-paid-100000-settle-harassment-claims-disgraced/story?id=51494871.

Flood, D. R. (2012). *Rape in Chicago: Race, Myth, and the Courts.* Chicago, Illinois, United States of America: Urbana: University of Illinois Press.

Foster, T. A. (September, 2011). The Sexual Abuse of Black Men under American Slavery. *Journal of the History of Sexuality, 20*(3), 445–46.

Fox, B., & DeLisi, M. (November, 2018). From criminological heterogeneity to coherent classes: developing a typology of juvenile sex offenders. *Youth Violence and Juvenile Justice, 16*(3), 299–318.

Freedman, E. (2013). *Redefining rape : sexual violence in the era of suffrage and segregation.* Cambridge, Massachusetts, United States of America: Harvard University Press.

Freedman, E. B. (August 24, 2012). *Women's Long Battle to Define Rape.* Retrieved December 15, 2019, from The Washington Post: https://www.washingtonpost.com/opinions/womens-long-battle-to-define-rape/2012/08/24/aa960280-ed34-11e1-a80b-9f898562d010_story.html.

Freeman, H. (January 26, 2018). *How was Larry Nassar able to abuse so many gymnasts for so long?* Retrieved March 24, 2018, from The Guardian: https://www.theguardian.com/sport/2018/jan/26/larry-nassar-abuse-gymnasts-scandal-culture.

Friedmann, G. (1946). Maurice Halbwachs, 1877-1945. *American Journal of Sociology,* 509–17.

Fuller, R., & Myers, R. (June 12, 1941). The Natural History of a Social Problem. *American Sociological Review, 6*(3), 320–29.

Gajanan, M. (May 21, 2016). *Bill Cosby's Sex Abuse Cases Ensnare Hugh Hefner.* Retrieved January 23, 2018, from Vanity Fair: Hive: https://www.vanityfair.com/news/2016/05/bill-cosbys-sex-abuse-cases-ensnare-hugh-hefner.

Gajanan, M. (January 4, 2018). *'There Is Strength in Numbers': Anthony Rapp Shares Why He Opened Up About Kevin Spacey.* Retrieved January 4, 2020, from Time: https://time.com/5088481/anthony-rapp-kevin-spacey-sexual-misconduct/.

Gajanan, M. (January 4, 2018). *'There Is Strength in Numbers': Anthony Rapp Shares Why He Opened Up About Kevin Spacey.* Retrieved January 4, 2020, from Time: https://time.com/5088481/anthony-rapp-kevin-spacey-sexual-misconduct/.

Garcia, S. E. (October 20, 2017). *The Woman Who Created #MeToo Long Before Hashtags.* Retrieved May 21, 2018, from The New York Times: https://www.nytimes.com/2017/10/20/us/me-too-movement-tarana-burke.html.

Gensburger, S. (2016). Halbwachs' studies in collective memory: A founding text for contemporary 'memory studies'? *Journal of Classical Sociology*, 396–413.

Gillespie, E., Mirabella, R., & Eikenberry, A. (2019). #Metoo/#Aidtoo and Creating an Intersectional Feminist NPO/NGO Secto. *Nonprofit Policy Forum*, 1–10.

Gillibrand, K. (June 30, 2019). *Gillibrand: The Military Justice Improvement Act would give service members a justice system that works*. Retrieved January 5, 2020, from Military Times: https://www.militarytimes.com/opinion/commentary/2019/06/30/gillibrand-the-military-justice-improvement-act-would-give-service-members-a-justice-system-that-works/.

Gilmore, A. K., Lewis, M. A., & George, W. H. (November 11, 2015). A randomized controlled trial targeting alcohol use and sexual assault risk among college women at high risk for victimization. *Behaviour Research and Therapy*, *74*, 38–49.

Glick, P., & Fiske, S. (2011). Ambivalent Sexism Revisited. *Psychology of Women Quarterly*, 530–535.

Glick, P., & Fiske, S. T. (1996). The ambivalent sexism inventory: Differentiating hostile and benevolent sexism. *Journal of Personality and Social Psychology*, *70*(3), 491–512.

Goldbaum, S., Craig, W., Pepler, D., & Connolly, J. (2003). Developmental trajectories of victimization . *Journal of Applied School Psychology*, *19*, 139–56.

Gravelin, C. R., Biernat, M., & Buche, C. E. (January 21, 2019). Blaming the Victim of Acquaintance Rape: Individual, Situational, and Sociocultural Factors. *Frontiers in Psychology*, *9*(2422), 1–22.

Green, E. L. (September 12, 2019). *Chicago Public Schools Ordered to Toughen Sexual Misconduct Policies*. Retrieved January 5, 2020, from The New York Times: https://www.nytimes.com/2019/09/12/us/politics/chicago-schools-sexual-misconduct.html.

Grimes, D. R. (September 22, 2014). *Alcohol is by far the most dangerous 'date rape drug'*. Retrieved November 10, 2017, from The Guardian: https://www.theguardian.com/science/blog/2014/sep/22/alcohol-date-rape-drug-facilitated-sexual-assault-dfsa.

Gross, S. J. (May 3, 2019). *Bill restricting citizen ballot initiatives nearly died. Now it heads to DeSantis*. Retrieved January 6, 2020, from Miami Herald: https://www.miamiherald.com/news/politics-government/state-politics/article230013339.html.

Groth, A. (1979). Sexual trauma in the life histories of rapists and child molesters. 4, 10–16. *Victimology: An International Journal*, *4*, 10–16.

Gqgabi, R. B., & Smit, E. I. (2019). Psycho-social effects of father–daughter incest: Views of South African social workers. *Journal of Child Sexual Abuse*, *28*(7), 840–859.

Guerra, K. (March 28, 2014). *Man drugged wife, made videos of raping her, suit says*. Retrieved November 18, 2017, from Indy Star: https://www.indystar.com/story/news/crime/2014/03/28/suit-accuses-ex-husband-drugs-rapes-sex-videos/7026395/?from=global&sessionKey=&autologin=.

Haggard, M. C., Kaelen, R., Saroglou, V., Klein, O., & Rowatt, W. C. (November, 2019). Religion's role in the illusion of gender equality: supraliminal and subliminal religious priming increases benevolent sexism. *Psychology of Religion and Spirituality, 11*(4), 392–8.

Hammond, M. D., Milojev, P., Huang, Y., & Sibley, C. G. (2018). Benevolent Sexism and Hostile Sexism Across the Ages. *Social Psychological and Personality Science, 9*(7), 863–74.

Harris, C. (December 19, 2017). *The Loathsome Den: Sexual Assault on the Plantation, #MeToo of the 19th century.* Retrieved December 9, 2019, from President Lincoln's Cottage: https://www.lincolncottage.org/the-loathsome-den-sexual-assault-on -the-plantation-metoo/.

Hartill, M. (2009). The Sexual Abuse of Boys in Organized Male Sports. *Men and Masculinities, 12*(2), 225–49.

Haskell, L., & Randall, M. (2019). *The Impact of Trauma on Adult Sexual Assault Victims.* Department of Justice Canada. Department of Justice Canada.

Hauslohner, A. (December 19, 2014). *Abigail Hauslohner: My friend raped me. Here is my story.* Retrieved November 17, 2017, from Dallas News: https://www.dallas news.com/opinion/commentary/2014/12/19/abigail-hauslohner-my-friend-raped -me.-here-is-my-story.

Hawks, L., Woolhandler, S., Himmelstein, D. U., Gaffney, A., & McCormick, D. (September 16, 2019). Association Between Forced Sexual Initiation and Health Outcomes Among US Women. *JAMA Internal Medicine , 179*(11), 1551–8.

Hendrix, J. A., Strom, K. J., Parish, W. J., Melton, P. A., & Young, A. R. (2020). An Examination of Sexual Assault Kit Submission Efficiencies Among a Nationally Representative Sample of Law Enforcement Agencies. *Criminal Justice Policy Review, 31*(7), 1095–115.

Hentschel, U. (2004). Defense Mechanisms : Theoretical, Research and Clinical Perspectives. *Advances in Psychology, 136,* 1–653.

Herman, D. (1988). The Rape Culture. *Culture, 1*(10), 45–53.

Hetherington, E. M., & Nunnally, M. (September, 2018). Access to the Civil Court System for Survivors ofChild Sexual Abuse in Georgia: Observations and Recommendations from the Clinical Legal Education Experience. *Georgia Law Review, 53.*

Hlavka, H. R. (June, 2014). Normalizing Sexual Violence: Young Women Account for Harassment and Abuse. *Gender & Society, 28*(3), 337–58.

Hobbs, T. D. (September 12, 2019). Chicago public schools agree to improve handling of sex-abuse complaints; department of education says system has long failed its students. *Wall Street Journal (Online).*

Hockett, J. M., Saucier, D. A., & Badke, C. (August 13, 2016). Rape Myths, Rape Scripts, and Common Rape Experiences of College Women: Differences in Perceptions of Women Who Have Been Raped. *Violence Against Women, 22*(3), 307–23.

Holland, K. J., & Cortina, L. M. (March, 2017). "It happens to girls all the time": Examining sexual assault survivors' reasons for not using campus supports. *American Journal of Community Psychology, 59*(1–2), 50–64.

Holloway, L. (January 4, 2016). *NewsOne*. Retrieved January 25, 2018, from 7 Celebrities Who Are Unapologetic In Their Support Of Bill Cosby: https://news one.com/3317134/seven-celebrities-support-bill-cosby/.

Holly, Y., McLaughlin, E. C., & Ford, D. (July 7, 2015). *Bill Cosby admitted to getting Quaaludes to give to women.* Retrieved January 18, 2018, from CNN: http://www.cnn.com/2015/07/07/us/bill-cosby-quaaludes-sexual-assault-allegations/index.html.

Horan, L., & Beauregard, E. (March 30, 2017). Pathways in the offending process of sex offenders who target marginalised victims. *Journal of Investigative Psychology and Offender Profiling, 14*(3), 213–26.

Hubbard, M. (March 31, 2014). *Sex offender therapy: A battle on multiple fronts.* Retrieved January 7, 2020, from Counseling Today: A Publication of the American Counseling Association: https://ct.counseling.org/2014/03/sex-offender-therapy-a-battle-on-multiple-fronts/.

Jackson, D., Marx, G., Perez Jr., J., & Smith Richards, J. (June 11, 2018). *Illinois law allows sex between teachers and students older than 17.* Retrieved January 5, 2020, from Chicago Tribute: http://graphics.chicagotribune.com/chicago-public-schools-sexual-abuse/amendola.

Jackson, D., Smith Richards, J., Marx, G., & Perez Jr., J. (July 28, 2018). *Betrayed: Chicago schools fail to protect students from sexual abuse and assault, leaving lasting damage.* Retrieved January 5, 2020, from Chicago Tribune: https://www.education dive.com/news/chicago-public-schools-violated-title-ix-for-systemic-failure-to-address/562825/.

Jesse, D. (March 15, 2019). *Courts ruling on side of students accused of sexual assault. Here's why.* Retrieved January 4, 2020, from Detroit Free Press: https://www.freep .com/story/news/education/2019/03/15/campus-sexual-assault-cases/3160325002/.

John Jay College of Criminal Justice. (2004). *The Nature and Scope of Sexual Abuse of Minors by Catholic Priests and Deacons in the United States 1950-2002.* The City University of New York, John Jay College of Criminal Justice. Washington, D.C: John Jay College of Criminal Justice.

Johnson, L. D. (September, 2018). Juvenile sex offenders: should they go to school with your children or should we create a pedophile academy. *University of Toledo Law Review, 50*(1), 39–65.

Joni Ernst United States Senator for Iowa (n.d.). *Combating Sexual Assault.* Retrieved January 3, 2020, from Joni Ernst United States Senator for Iowa: https://www. ernst.senate.gov/public/index.cfm/combating.

Joyal, C. C., Carpentier, J., & Martin, C. (2016). Discriminant factors for adolescent sexual offending: on the usefulness of considering both victim age and sibling incest. *Child Abuse & Neglect, 54*, 10–22.

Kaiser, K., O'Neal, E., & Spohn, C. (April, 2017). Victim Refuses to Cooperate": A Focal Concerns Analysis of Victim Cooperation in Sexual Assault Cases. *Victims & Offenders*, *12*(2), 297–322.

Kantor, J., & Twohey, M. (2019). *She Said: Breaking the Sexual Harassment Story That Helped Ignite a Movement*. New York, NY, U.S.A.: Penguin Press.

Kaukinen, C., & DeMaris, A. (2005). Age at first sexual assault and current substance use and depression. *Journal of Interpersonal Violence*, *20*(10), 1244–270.

Kim, K., Littlefield, C., & Etehad, M. (June 17, 2017). *Timeline Bill Cosby: A 50-year chronicle of accusations and accomplishments*. Retrieved January 18, 2018, from LA Times: http://www.latimes.com/entertainment/la-et-bill-cosby-timeline-html story.html.

King, A. S. (June 13, 2017). *Blame It on the . . . Quaaludes? Guilty or Not, Bill Cosby Still Preferred Sex With Intoxicated Women*. Retrieved January 18, 2018, from The Root: https://www.theroot.com/blame-it-on-the-quaaludes-guilty-or-not-bill -cosby-1796063880.

Kingdon, J. W. (2010). *Agendas, alternatives, and public policies* (2nd Edition ed.). New York, NY, United States of America: Pearson.

Kingkade, T. (October 8, 2014). *Texas Tech Frat Loses Charter Following 'No Means Yes, Yes Means Anal' Display*. Retrieved January 2, 2020, from Huffington Post: https://www.huffpost.com/entry/texas-tech-frat-no-means-yes_n_5953302.

Kingkade, T. (March 8, 2016). *He Admitted To Sexual Assault, But She's The One They Tried To Silence*. Retrieved December 20, 2019, from Huffington Post: https:// www.huffpost.com/entry/college-sexual-assault-gag-orders_n_56ddd17ae4b0ffe6f 8ea278c.

Kingkade, T. (April 13, 2017). *Meet the teen sexual assault survivors who took on their school district and won*. Retrieved April 5, 2021, from Buzz Feed News: https:// www.buzzfeednews.com/article/tylerkingkade/high-schoolers-are-ready-for-these -conversations.

Kitch, S. (2009). *The specter of sex: gendered foundations of racial formation in the United States*. Albany, New York, United States of America: State University of New York Pres.

Kitchener, C. (August 26, 2019). *The Lily*. Retrieved April 4, 2021, from She reported her sexual assault. Her high school suspended her for 'sexual impropriety.': https://www.thelily.com/she-reported-her-sexual-assault-her-high-school -suspended-her-for-sexual-impropriety/.

Kruger, T., Sinke, C., Kneer, J., Tenbergen, G., Qayyum, K., Burkert, A., . . . (2019). Child sexual offenders show prenatal and epigenetic alterations of the androgen system. *Translational Psychiatry*, 28.

La Bash, H., & Papa, A. (March 1, 2014). Shame and PTSD symptoms. *Psychological Trauma: Theory, Research, Practice, and Policy*, *6*(2), 159–66.

Lahav, Y., Ginzburg, K., & Spiegel, D. (June 27, 2019). Post-Traumatic Growth, Dissociation, and Sexual Revictimization in Female Childhood Sexual Abuse Survivors. *Child Maltreatment*, *25*(1), 96–105.

Langton, C., Barbaree, H., Harkins, L., Arenovich, T., Mcnamee, J., Peacock, E., . . . Marcon, H. (2008). Denial and minimization among sexual offenders. *Criminal Justice and Behavior, 35*(1), 69–98.

Lara, S., & Meyer, I. H. (June, 2014). The Sexual Victimization of Men in America: New Data Challenge Old Assumptions. *American Journal of Public Health, 104*(6), 19–26.

Laughlin, K. (September , 2018). *What Puts Survivors at Increased Risk for Suicide and How to Help.* Retrieved January 2, 2020, from National Sexual Violence Resource Center (NSVRC): https://www.nsvrc.org/blogs/what-puts-survivors -increased-risk-suicide-and-how-help.

Leone, H. (November 22, 2019). *Hundreds of new sex abuse or misconduct allegations involving CPS students reported since September. 'What can we do to prevent this?'* Retrieved January 5, 2020, from Chicago Tribune: https://www.chicagotribune .com/news/breaking/ct-chicago-public-schools-sexual-abuse-investigations-up date-20191122-3mccxmsd5rh2filslmkrkhorbe-story.html.

Leone, H., & Jackson, D. (September 12, 2019). *'Extraordinary and appalling' handling of sexual violence cases in Chicago Public Schools leads to federal oversight.* Retrieved December 13, 2020, from The Chicago Tribune: https://www.chicagotribune.com /news/breaking/ct-chicago-public-schools-federal-resolution-sexual-misconduct -20190912-c74uguy67rd4pp2dyjgfr647u4-story.html.

Levenson, E. (May 17, 2018). *Michigan State University reaches $500 million settlement with Larry Nassar victims.* Retrieved May 21, 2018, from CNN: https://www.cnn .com/2018/05/16/us/larry-nassar-michigan-state-settlement/index.html.

Levenson, E., & Cooper, A. (April 26, 2018). *Bill Cosby guilty on all three counts in indecent assault trial.* Retrieved May 21, 2018, from CNN: https://www.cnn .com/2018/04/26/us/bill-cosby-trial/index.html.

Levenson, E., del Valle, L., & Moghe, S. (March 11, 2020). *Harvey Weinstein sentenced to 23 years in prison after addressing his accusers in court.* Retrieved April 14, 2021, from CNN: https://www.cnn.com/2020/03/11/us/harvey-weinstein -sentence/index.html.

Leversee, T. (March 1, 2017). *Chapter 2: Etiology and Typologies of Juveniles Who Have Committed Sexual Offenses.* (M. A. Office of Sex Offender Sentencing, Producer) Retrieved March 20, 2021, from Sex Offender Management Assessment and Planning Initiative : https://smart.ojp.gov/somapi/chapter-2-etiology-and -typologies-juveniles-who-have-committed-sexual-offenses.

Levy, M. (June 8, 2016). *'Hero' students tackled Brock Turner after Stanford University rape.* Retrieved December 20, 2019, from Sydney Morning Herald: https://www .smh.com.au/world/hero-students-tackled-brock-turner-after-stanford-university -rape-20160608-gpdz5v.html.

Limining, S. (March 24, 2017). *The Silencing of Sexual Violence Survivors.* Retrieved April 11, 2021, from Inside Higher Ed: https://www.insidehighered.com/advice /2017/03/24/trouble-nondisclosure-agreements-sexual-assault-cases-essay.

Lisak, D. (2002). *Undetected Rapists.* University of Massachusetts, Psychology, Boston.

Lisak, D. (2008). Understanding the Predatory Nature of Sexual Violence. 1–12.

Lisak, D. (January 3, 2008). *Government Innovators Network*. Retrieved September 8, 2020, from Harvard Kennedy School: https://www.innovations.harvard.edu /understanding-predatory-nature-sexual-violence.

Lisak, D., & Miller, P. (2002). Repeat rape and multiple offending among undetected rapists. *Violence and Victims, 17*, 73–84.

Lockett, D. (June 8, 2017). *These Are the Celebrities Bill Cosby Has Brought With Him to His Sexual-Assault Trial*. Retrieved January 25, 2018, from Vulture: http://www .vulture.com/2017/06/all-the-celebrities-bill-cosby-has-brought-to-his-trial.html.

Lombardo, K. (June 9, 2016). *How a rape case involving a Stanford swimmer became national news*. Retrieved December 20, 2019, from Sports Illustrated: https://www .si.com/more-sports/brock-turner-stanford-swimming-sexual-assault-rape-case.

Lombardo, K. (June 9, 2016). *How a rape case involving a Stanford swimmer became national news*. Retrieved December 20, 2019, from Sports Illustrated: https://www .si.com/more-sports/brock-turner-stanford-swimming-sexual-assault-rape-case.

Loofbourow, L. (May 30, 2019). *Why Society Goes Easy on Rapists*. Retrieved January 5, 2020, from Slate: https://slate.com/news-and-politics/2019/05/sexual-assault -rape-sympathy-no-prison.html.

Lyons, J. D. (June 16, 2016). *What Judge Aaron Persky Said About Brock Turner During His Sentencing Hearing Will Appall You*. Retrieved December 20, 2019, from Bustle: https://www.bustle.com/articles/167321-what-judge-aaron-persky-said-about -brock-turner-during-his-sentencing-hearing-will-appall-you.

Magness, J. (October 18, 2017). *'It didn't end': Olympian McKayla Maroney said US team doctor first molested her at 13*. Retrieved March 24, 2018, from Miami Herald: http://www.miamiherald.com/news/nation-world/national/article179476911 .html.

Margari, F., Lecce, P. A., Craig, F., Lafortezza, E., Lisi, A., Pinto, F., . . . Grattagliano, I. (September 30, 2015). Juvenile sex offenders: personality profile, coping styles and parental care. *Psychiatry Research, 229*(1–2), 82–88.

Margulies, J. (September 6, 2016). *Racism, Classism, Feminism . . . and Brock Turner*. Retrieved December 20, 2019, from Verdict: https://verdict.justia.com/2016/09/06 /racism-classism-feminism-brock-turner.

Marques, J. K., Wiederanders, M., Day, D. M., Nelson, C., & van Ommeren, A. (January, 200). Effects of a relapse prevention program on sexual recidivism: final results from California's sex offender treatment and evaluation project (SOTEP). *Sexual Abuse: A Journal of Research and Treatment: Official Journal of the Association for the Treatment of Sexual Abusers, 17*(1), 79–107.

Mary, S., & Senn, P. (1995). What is a Social Problem? A History of its Definition. (N. M. Klingemann C., Ed.) *Jahrbuch für Soziologiegeschichte 1993*.

Masterson, M. (Janauary 6, 2020). *CPS Watchdog Opened 450 New Sexual Misconduct Investigations in 2019*. Retrieved September 13, 2020, from WTTW: https://news .wttw.com/2020/01/06/cps-watchdog-opened-450-new-sexual-misconduct-inves tigations-2019.

McCoy, K. (February 5, 2015). *What Does the Bible Say About Sexual Assault?* Retrieved November 29, 2017, from Biblical Woman: http://biblicalwoman.com /bible-sexual-assault-women/.

McCrummen, S., Reinhard, B., & Crites, A. (November 9, 2017). *Washington Post*. Retrieved November 17, 2017, from Woman says Roy Moore initiated sexual encounter when she was 14, he was 32: https://www.washingtonpost.com /investigations/woman-says-roy-moore-initiated-sexual-encounter-when-she -was-14-he-was-32/2017/11/09/1f495878-c293-11e7-afe9-4f60b5a6c4a0_story .html?utm_term=.cae522ec3e04.

McCuish, E. C., & Lussier, P. (November, 2017). Unfinished stories: from juvenile sex offenders to juvenile sex offending through a developmental life course perspective. *Aggression and Violent Behavior*, 37, 71–82.

McDonald, S. N. (November 21, 2014). *Two new Cosby accusers emerge, including former Playboy bunny Carla Ferrigno*. Retrieved January 18, 2018, from The Washington Post: https://www.washingtonpost.com/news/morning-mix/wp/2014 /11/21/two-new-cosby-accusers-emerge-including-former-playboy-bunny-carla -ferrigno/?utm_term=.a08bd315d6c2.

McDowell, M. G. (2015). Virtuous icons: Priests as unique persons or gendered stereotypes? *Greek Orthodox Theological Review*, 60(1/2), 143–63.

McLaughlin, K. (August 27, 2019). *After a Georgia teenager reported a sexual assault to her school administrators, she says she was expelled for 'sexual impropriety.' Now she's suing*. Retrieved April 10, 2020, from Insider: https://www.insider.com/fayette -county-board-of-education-sued-reported-sexual-assault-2019-8.

McMahon, S., & Farmer, G. L. (June, 2011). An Updated Measure for Assessing Subtle Rape Myths. *Social Work Research*, 35(2), 71–81.

Meek, J. G., Sisk, R., Bazinet, K. R., McAuliff, M., & Schapiro, R. (March 11, 2010). *Disgraced ex-Rep. Eric Massa's long trail of bizarre behavior includes home shared with staffers*. Retrieved December 20, 2019, from Daily News: https://www.nydaily news.com/news/politics/disgraced-ex-rep-eric-massa-long-trail-bizarre-behavior -includes-home-shared-staffers-article-1.164192.

Mensching, C. (January 31, 2006). *Molester sentenced to 74 years in prison*. Retrieved April 7, 2021, from Redlands Daily Facts: https://www.redlandsdailyfacts.com /2006/01/31/molester-sentenced-to-74-years-in-prison/.

Mercado, C., Tallon, J., & Terry, K. (May 1, 2008). Persistent sexual abusers in the Catholic Church. *Criminal Justice and Behavior*, 35(5), 629–42.

Michael, L. (November 29, 2017). *Hypermasculinity Is A Plague On The Modern Man*. Retrieved June 29, 2018, from Huffington Post: https://www.huffingtonpost.co.uk /louis-michael/hyper-masculinity-man_b_13280034.html?guccounter=1.

Middleton, W. (2013). Ongoing Incestuous Abuse During Adulthood. *Journal of Trauma & Dissociation*, 14(3), 251–72.

Middleton, W. (2013). Ongoing Incestuous Abuse During Adulthood. *Journal of Trauma & Dissociation*, 14(3), 251–72.

Modan, N. (September 12, 2019). *Chicago Public Schools violated Title IX for 'systemic failure' to address student sexual violence claims.* Retrieved January 5, 2020, from Education Dive: https://www.educationdive.com/news/chicago-public-schools -violated-title-ix-for-systemic-failure-to-address/562825/.

Moghe, S. (July 25, 2015). *Cosby deposition: Quaaludes came from L.A. gynecologist.* Retrieved January 18, 2018, from CNN: http://www.cnn.com/2015/07/24/us/cosby -deposition-quaaludes/index.html.

Moles, R., & Leventhal, J. (2014). Sexual abuse and assault in children and teens: time to prioritize prevention. . *The Journal of Adolescent Health: Official Publication of the Society for Adolescent Medicine, 312*–13.

Moles, R., & Leventhal, J. (2014). Sexual abuse and assault in children and teens: time to prioritize prevention. . *The Journal of Adolescent Health: Official Publication of the Society for Adolescent Medicine, 312*–13.

Monahan, J., & Polk, S. (January 6, 2020). *The Effect of Cultural Bias on the Investigation and Prosecution of Sexual Assault.* Retrieved January 6, 2020, from International Association of Chiefs of Police: Police Chief: https://www.policechiefmaga zine.org/the-effect-of-cultural-bias-on-the-investigation/.

Moniuszko, S. M., & Kelly, C. (October 27, 2017). *Harvey Weinstein scandal: A complete list of the 84 accusers.* Retrieved January 8, 2018, from USA Today: https:// www.usatoday.com/story/life/people/2017/10/27/weinstein-scandal-complete-list -accusers/804663001/.

Monk-Turner, E., & Light, D. (2010). Male sexual assault and rape: who seeks counseling? *Sexual Abuse: A Journal of Research and Treatment, 22*(3), 255–65.

Moon, S., & Reger, J. (2014). You are not your own: Rape, Sexual Assault, and Consent in Evangelical Christian Dating Books. *Journal of Integrated Social Sciences, 4*(1), 55–74.

Morabito, A. (July 20, 2017). *'Mattress Girl' case: Man falsely accused of rape wins settlement from Columbia.* Retrieved January 3, 2020, from Washington Examiner: https://www.washingtonexaminer.com/red-alert-politics/mattress-girl-case-man -falsely-accused-rape-wins-settlement-columbia.

Moynihan, M. M., & Banyard, V. L. (October 11, 2008). Community responsibility for preventing sexual violence: A pilot study with campus Greeks and intercollegiate athletes. *Journal of Prevention & Intervention in the Community, 36*(1–2), 23–38.

Muldoon, S. D., Taylor, S. C., & Norma, C. (2016). The survivor master narrative in sexual assault. *Violence against Women, 22*(5), 565–87.

National Center for Fathering. (2018). *The Extent of Fatherlessness.* Retrieved June 11, 201, from National Center for Fathering: http://www.fathers.com/statistics-and -research/the-extent-of-fatherlessness/.

National Institute of Justice. (January 6, 2020). *Practice Profile Adult Sex Offender Treatment.* Retrieved January 6, 2020, from Crime Solutions: https://www.crime solutions.gov/PracticeDetails.aspx?ID=30.

National Sexual Violence Resource Center. (September 1, 2013). *Engaging Bystanders to Prevent Sexual Violence: A Guide for Preventionists.* Retrieved January 6, 2020, from National Sexual Violence Resource Center: https://www.nsvrc.org/sites/default /files/2013-09/publications_nsvrc_guide_engaging-bystanders-prevent-sexual -violence_0.pdf.

National Sexual Violence Resource Center. (September, 2018). *Teenagers & Sexual Violence.* Retrieved March 28, 2021, from National Sexual Violence Resource Center: https://www.nsvrc.org/sites/default/files/publications/2019-02/Teenagers _508.pdf.

National Women's Law Center. (August 23, 2019). *NWLC Sues Georgia High School for Expelling Student Who Reported She Was Sexually Assaulted After School.* Retrieved April 5, 2021, from NWLC: https://nwlc.org/press-releases/nwlc -sues-georgia-high-school-for-expelling-student-who-reported-she-was-sexually -assaulted-after-school/.

National Women's Law Center. (August 23, 2019). *NWLC Sues Georgia High School for Expelling Student Who Reported She Was Sexually Assaulted After School.* Retrieved April 5, 2021, from NWLC: https://nwlc.org/press-releases/nwlc -sues-georgia-high-school-for-expelling-student-who-reported-she-was-sexually -assaulted-after-school/.

Newport, F. (2017). *2017 Update on Americans and Religion.* Gallup, Gallup U.S. Daily Works. Washington, D.C.: Gallop.

North, A. (January 26, 2019). *Sen. Joni Ernst has become one of the most prominent Republicans to say she's been sexually assaulted.* Retrieved January 3, 2020, from Vox: https://www.vox.com/2019/1/26/18196180/joni-ernst-gail-divorce-kavanaugh -vote-vp.

Nyren, E. (October 29, 2017). *Rose McGowan Says Harvey Weinstein Offered Her $1 Million to Sign NDA (Report).* Retrieved January 3, 2020, from Variety: https://variety.com/2017/biz/news/rose-mcgowan-harvey-weinstein-hush-money -1202601910/.

O'Donohue, W., Benuto, L., Fondren, R., Tolle, L., & Vijay, A. &. (October, 2013). Dimensions of child sexual abuse allegations: what is unusual and what is not? *Journal of Forensic Psychology Practice, 13*(5), 456–75.

Office of Justice Program. (January 6, 2020). *Office for Victims of Crime Training & Technical Assistance Center.* Retrieved January 6, 2020, from DNA in Sexual Assault Cases: The Role of Law Enforcement, SAFE/SANE Nurses, and Victim Advocates: https://www.ovcttac.gov/views/TrainingMaterials/dspDNACollec tion.cfm.

Okur, P., Pereda, N., Van Der Knaap, L. M., & Bogaerts, S. (2019). Attributions of Blame among Victims of Child Sexual Abuse: Findings from a Community Sample. Journal of Child Sexual Abuse, 28(3), 301–17.

Olivier, A. (January 13, 2015). *Bill Cosby, His Accusers And The Way We Treat Women Who Say They Are Victims Of Sexual Assault.* Retrieved January 18, 2018, from Madamenoire: http://madamenoire.com/502281/victims-of-sexual-assault/.

Orlando, C. J. (September 29, 2016). *How Society Is Raising Rapists—A Man's Perspective*. Retrieved June 6, 2018, from Huffington Post: https://www.huffingtonpost.com/entry/how-society-is-raising-rapistsa-mans-perspective_us_57e4b061e4b09f67131e4012.

Our Resilience. (January, 2020). *Sexual Violence Myths & Facts*. Retrieved January 11, 2020, from Our Resilience: https://www.ourresilience.org/what-you-need-to-know/myths-and-facts/.

Page, A. D. (October, 2010). True Colors: Police Officers and Rape Myth Acceptance. *Feminist Criminology, 5*(4), 315–34.

Papalia, N., Luebbers, S., Ogloff, J., Cutajar, M., Mullen, P., & Mann, E. (April, 2017). Further victimization of child sexual abuse victims: a latent class typology of re-victimization trajectories. *Child Abuse & Neglect, 66*, 112–29.

Papalia, N., Mann, E., & Ogloff, J. (June 23, 2020). Child sexual abuse and risk of revictimization: impact of child demographics, sexual abuse characteristics, and psychiatric disorders. *Child Maltreatment, 26*(1), 74–86.

Patterson, D. (2011). The impact of detectives' manner of questioning on rape victims' disclosure. *Violence against Women, 17*(11), 1349–73.

Pazzani, L. M. (July 13, 2007). The factors affecting sexual assaults committed by strangers and acquaintances. *Violence against Women, 13*(7), 717–49.

Pearl, D. (October 8, 2016). *A Complete Timeline of the Nate Parker Rape Allegations and the Production of Birth of a Nation*. Retrieved July 3, 2018, from People: https://people.com/movies/a-complete-timeline-of-the-nate-parker-rape-allegations-and-the-production-of-birth-of-a-nation/.

Perillo, A., Mercado, C., & Terry, K. (May 1, 2008). Repeat Offending, Victim Gender, and Extent of Victim Relationship in Catholic Church Sexual Abusers. *Criminal Justice and Behavior, 35*(5), 600–14.

Pesce, N. L. (October 4, 2018). *The #MeToo movement has changed policies across industries, but there's still work to be done*. Retrieved January 4, 2020, from Market Watch: https://www.marketwatch.com/story/the-metoo-movement-has-changed-policies-across-industries-but-theres-still-work-to-be-done-2018-10-04.

Phipps, A. (June 6, 2018). Reckoning up: Sexual harassment and violence in the neoliberal university. *Gender and Education, 32*(2), 227–243.

Phipps, A. (2020). *Me, Not You : The Trouble with Mainstream Feminism*. Manchester: Manchester University Press.

Pilgrim, D. (November 2, 2000). *The Brute Caricature*. Retrieved December 9, 2019, from Ferris State University: Jim Crow Museum: https://www.ferris.edu/jimcrow/brute/.

Pilgrim, D. (July 1, 2002). *The Jezebel Stereotype*. Retrieved December 16, 2019, from Ferris State University: Jim Crow Museum of Racist Memorabilia: https://www.ferris.edu/HTMLS/news/jimcrow/jezebel/index.htm.

Pittenger, S., Huit, T., & Hansen, D. (2016). Applying ecological systems theory to sexual revictimization of youth: A review with implications for research and practice. *Aggression and Violent Behavior, 26*, 35–45.

Pollack, D. (November , 2015). *Understanding Sexual Grooming in Child Abuse Cases*. Retrieved November 27, 2019, from American Bar Association: https://www .americanbar.org/groups/public_interest/child_law/resources/child_law_practice online/child_law_practice/vol-34/november-2015/understanding-sexual-groom ing-in-child-abuse-cases/.

Prina, F., & Schatz-Stevens, J. (2020). Sexism and rape myth acceptance: The impact of culture, education, and religiosity. *Psychological Report*, 929–51.

Przybylski, R., & Lobanov-Rostovsky, C. (January 1, 2020). *Chapter 1: Unique Considerations Regarding Juveniles Who Commit Sexual Offenses*. (U.S. Department of Justice: Office of Justice Programs) Retrieved January 10, 2020, from Office of Sex Offender Sentencing, Monitoring, Apprehending, Registering, and Tracking: https://smart.ojp.gov/somapi/chapter-1-unique-considerations-regarding-juveniles -who-commit-sexual-offenses.

Puente, M. (November 25, 2019). *Bill Cosby interview: He expects to serve full 10-year sentence rather than say 'sorry'*. Retrieved April 14, 2021, from USA Today: https:// www.usatoday.com/story/entertainment/celebrities/2019/11/25/bill-cosby-expects -serve-full-sentence-rather-than-say-sorry/4299623002/.

Puente, M. (December 7, 2021). *Harvey Weinstein's Los Angeles sex-crime case lives on; Rose McGowan's civil suit against him thrown out*. Retrieved from USA Today: https://www.usatoday.com/story/entertainment/celebrities/2021/12/07/harvey -weinstein-la-sex-crime-case-lives-on-rose-mcgowan-suit-over/6421171001/.

Pullman, E. S. (May, 2017). Differences between biological and sociolegal incest offenders: A meta-analysis. *Aggression and Violent Behavior*, 34, Pages 228–37.

RAINN. (December 20, 2019,). *Telling Loved Ones About Sexual Assault*. Retrieved January 1, 2020, from RAINN (Rape, Abuse & Incest National Network): https:// www.rainn.org/articles/telling-loved-ones-about-sexual-assault.

RAINN. (March 7, 2018). *Children and Teens: Statistics*. Retrieved January 6, 2020, from RAINN (Rape, Abuse, Incest, National Network): https://www.rainn.org /statistics/children-and-teens.

RAINN. (January, 2020). *RAINN (Rape, Abuse, Incest, National Network)*. Retrieved January 11, 2020, from Scope of the Problem: Statistics: https://www.rainn.org /statistics/scope-problem.

Ramirez, S. R., Jeglic, E. L., & Calkins, C. (June 24, 2015). An examination of the relationship between childhood abuse, anger and violent behavior among a sample of sex offenders. *Health & Justice*, 3(14), 1–6.

Randol, B. M., & Sanders, C. M. (2015). Examining the barriers to sexual assault evidence processing in Washington state: What's the hold up? *Criminology, Criminal Justice, Law & Society*, 16, 1–13.

Rape Victim Advocates. (January 28, 2018). *Sexual Violence Myths & Facts*. Retrieved June 12, 2018, from Rape Victim Advocates: https://www.rapevictimadvocates .org/what-you-need-to-know/myths-and-facts/.

Rape, Abuse, & Incest National Network. (January 2, 2018). *The Criminal Justice System: Statistics*. Retrieved June 12, 2018, from Rape, Abuse, & Incest National Network: https://www.rainn.org/statistics/criminal-justice-system

Rape, Abuse, Incest National Network [RAINN]. (January 17, 2020). *Campus Sexual Violence: Statistics*. Retrieved April 11, 2021, from RAINN: https://www.rainn.org/statistics/campus-sexual-violence

Raphael, J. (2013). *Rape Is Rape : How Denial, Distortion, and Victim Blaming Are Fueling a Hidden Acquaintance Rape Crisis*. Chicago, Illinois, United States of America: Independent Publishers Group.

Redden, M. (December 14, 2017). *The Rape of Recy Taylor: behind one of the year's most vital documentaries*. Retrieved December 15, 2019, from The Guardian: https://www.theguardian.com/film/2017/dec/14/the-of-recy-taylor-behind-one-of-the-years-most-vital-documentaries.

Reilly, K. (May 24, 2016). *Here's What Makes This Accusation Against Bill Cosby Different From Others*. Retrieved January 25, 2018, from Time: U.S. Courts: http://time.com/4346387/bill-cosby-andrea-constand-sex-assault-accusation/

Reingold, R. (December 20, 2017). *#MeToo: Who is Being Left Out?* Retrieved from O'Neill Institute Georgetown Law: https://oneill.law.georgetown.edu/metoo-who-is-being-left-out/.

Relyea, M., & Ullman, S. E. (October, 2017). Predicting sexual assault revictimization in a longitudinal sample of women survivors: variation by type of assault. *Violence against Women, 23*(12), 1462–1483.

Rentoul, L., & Appleboom, N. (August, 1997). Understanding the psychological impact of rape and serious sexual assault of men: a literature review. *Journal of Psychiatric Mental Health Nursing, 4*(4), 267V74.

Rhodan, M. (July 16, 2016). *Why Are Quaaludes the Drugs Bill Cosby Used?* Retrieved January 18, 2018, from Time: http://time.com/3947705/quaaludes-bill-cosby/.

Richards, T. (July 10, 2016). An Updated Review of Institutions of Higher Education's Responses to Sexual Assault: Results From a Nationally Representative Sample. *Journal of Interpersonal Violence, 34*(10), 1983–2012.

Right 2 Consent. (March, 2021). *Report It: Questionnaire for Law Enforcement Interview*. Retrieved April 15, 2021, from Right 2 Consent: https://right2consent.com/#report

Rios, E. (January 29, 2018). *Larry Nassar Is Locked Up for Life, But Michigan State's Trouble Is Just Starting*. Retrieved March 24, 2018, from Mother Jones: https://www.motherjones.com/crime-justice/2018/01/larry-nassar-is-locked-up-for-life-but-michigan-states-trouble-is-just-starting/.

Robertiello, G., & Terry, K. J. (September, 2007). Can we profile sex offenders? a review of sex offender typologies. *Aggression and Violent Behavior, 12*(5), 508–518.

Roberts, K. (October 6, 2016). *The Psychology of Victim-Blaming*. Retrieved January 11, 2020, from The Atlantic: https://www.theatlantic.com/science/archive/2016/10/the-psychology-of-victim-blaming/502661/.

Rollero, C., & Tartaglia, S. (2019). The effect of sexism and rape myths on victim blame. *Sexuality and Culture*, 209–219.

Rosenbaum, C. (March 8, 2016). *Bill Cosby's Wife Refused To Answer At Least 98 Questions Under Oath*. Retrieved January 23, 2018, from Buzzfeed: https://www .buzzfeed.com/claudiarosenbaum/camille-cosby-wife-cites-marital-privilege-under -oath?utm_term=.ktNz1GGedZ#.ihV8KxxmoV

Rowan, E. L. (2006). *Understanding Child Sexual Abuse (Understanding Health and Sickness Series)*. Jackson, Mississippi, United States of America: University Press of Mississippi.

Rufo, R. A. (2011). *Sexual Predators Amongst Us*. Boca Raton, FL, U.S.A.: CRC Press LLC.

Ryan, L. (October 5, 2018). *Our Year of Reckoning: An Exhaustive Timeline*. Retrieved December 30, 2019, from The Cut: https://www.thecut.com/2018/10/sexual -harassment-harvey-weinstein-allegations.html

Saad, N. (October 4, 2017). *Gabrielle Union recounts struggles with infertility and a college rape*. Retrieved November 18, 2017, from LA Times: http://www.latimes.com /entertainment/la-et-entertainment-news-updates-gabrielle-union-miscarriages -rape-memoir-1507152688-htmlstory.html

Saad, N. (September 9, 2019). *How the N.Y. Times got Ashley Judd and other Weinstein victims to talk*. Retrieved January 4, 2020, from Los Angeles Times: https://www .latimes.com/entertainment-arts/tv/story/2019-09-09/ashley-judd-weinstein-today -show-she-said

Sabatier, P. A., & Weible, C. M. (April 9, 2014). *Theories of the Policy Process* (Vol. 3). Boulder, Colorado: Westview Press. Retrieved January 3, 2020.

Sailofsky, D. (2019). When rape was legal—the untold history of sexual violence during slavery. *Sociological Inquiry*, 89(3), 556.

Sampson, R. (2013). *Acquaintance Rape of College Students*. Community of Oriented Policing Services, Center for Problem Oriented Policing. Washington: U.S. Department of Justice.

Santhanam, L. (September 16, 2019). *1 in 16 U.S. women say their first sexual intercourse was rape*. Retrieved January 12, 2020, from PBS News Hour: https://www .pbs.org/newshour/health/1-in-16-u-s-women-say-their-first-sexual-intercourse -was-rape

Scales Rostosky, S., Dekhtyar, O., Cupp, P. K., & Anderman, E. M. (September 13, 2016). Sexual Self-Concept and Sexual Self-Efficacy in Adolescents: A Possible Clue to Promoting Sexual Health? *Journal of Sex Research*, 45(3), 277–286.

School Counseling By Heart (August 26, 2012). *Teaching Kids to Recognize Grooming*. Retrieved January 6, 2020, from School Counseling By Heart: https://www .schoolcounselingbyheart.com/2012/08/26/teaching-kids-to-recognize-grooming/

Schulte, S. (June 1, 2018). *Chicago Tribune report finds 500 cases of sexual abuse, rape in CPS schools over 10 years*. Retrieved January 5, 2020, from ABC 7: https:// abc7chicago.com/chicago-tribune-report-finds-500-cases-of-sexual-abuse-rape-in -cps-schools-over-10-years/3549912/

Seto, M., Babchishin, K., Pullman, L., & McPhail, I. (April 17, 2015). The puzzle of intrafamilial child sexual abuse: a meta-analysis comparing intrafamilial and extrafamilial offenders with child victims. *Clinical Psychology Review, 39,* 42–57.

Setoodeh, R. (October 5, 2015). *Ashley Judd Reveals Sexual Harassment by Studio Mogul (Exclusive).* Retrieved January 4, 2020, from Variety: https://variety.com/2015/film/news/ashley-judd-sexual-harassment-studio-mogul-shower-1201610666/

Shapiro, E. (September 24, 2019). *'Humiliated': Chanel Miller, survivor in Brock Turner sex assault case, shares her story of trauma and recovery.* Retrieved December 20, 2019, from ABC News: https://abcnews.go.com/US/humiliated-chanel-miller-survivor-brock-turner-sex-assault/story?id=65821466

Shattuck, A., Finkelhor, D., Turner, H., & Hamby, S. (February, 2016). Children exposed to abuse in youth-serving organizations: Results from national sample surveys. *Jama Pediatrics, 170*(2).

Sheley, E. (April 13, 2018). Broken windows theory of sexual assault enforcement. *Journal of Criminal Law and Criminology, 108*(3), 455–510.

Shendruk, A., & Ossola, A. (September 11, 2019). *The memo from Harvey Weinstein's lawyer is a roadmap for how accused predators stay in power.* Retrieved January 4, 2020, from Quartz: https://qz.com/1707143/lisa-blooms-memo-to-harvey-weinstein-is-a-roadmap-for-abusers/

Shepard, J. M. (2012). *Sociology* (11th Edition ed.). Belmont, CA, U.S.A.: Cengage Learning, Inc.

Sigurvinsdottir, R., & Ullman, S. E. (October, 2016). Sexual orientation, race, and trauma as predictors of sexual assault recovery. *Journal of Family Violence, 31*(7), 913–21.

Simons, D. (January 1, 2020). *Chapter 3: Sex Offender Typologies.* Retrieved September 24, 2020, from Office of Sex Offender Sentencing, Monitoring, Apprehending, Registering, and Tracking (SMART): https://smart.ojp.gov/somapi/chapter-3-sex-offender-typologies#refe

Sjöberg, M., & Sarwar, F. (2020). Who Gets Blamed for Rapes: Effects of Immigration Status on the Attribution of Blame Toward Victims and Perpetrators. *Journal of Interpersonal Violence,* 2446–246.

Slusser, R. (May 25, 2015). *My father raped his daughter. And I am their baby. My story.* Retrieved November 17, 2017, from Life Site: https://www.lifesitenews.com/opinion/i-was-conceived-when-my-father-raped-his-daughter.-should-i-have-been-abort

Smith, T. (October 5, 2019). *Is Redemption Possible In The Aftermath Of #MeToo?* Retrieved January 3, 2020, from NPR: https://www.npr.org/2019/10/05/766843292/is-redemption-possible-in-the-aftermath-of-metoo

Smith-Kimble, C. (January 21, 2021). *The Realities of Sexual Assault on Campus.* Retrieved April 11, 2021, from Best Colleges: https://www.bestcolleges.com/resources/sexual-assault-on-campus/

Sneed, W. (2018). *A Report of the History and Mode of Management of the Kentucky Penitentiary, from Its Origin, in 1798, to March 1, 1860 (Classic Reprint)* (Vol. 4). London, England: Forgotten Books.

Spohn, C., & Holleran, D. (2004). *Prosecuting Sexual Assault: A Comparison of Charging Decisions in Sexual Assault Cases Involving Strangers, Acquaintances, and Intimate Partners.* National Institute of Justice, Office of Justice Programs, U.S. Department of Justice. District of Columbia: National Institute of Justice,.

Stander, V. A., Thomsen, C. J., Merrill, L. L., & Milner, J. S. (May 4, 2018). Longitudinal prediction of sexual harassment and sexual assault by male enlisted navy personnel. *Military Psychology, 30*(3).

Stateside Staff (January 23, 2018). *Legal expert examines MSU's potential civil and criminal liabilities in Nassar scandal.* Retrieved March 24, 2018, from Michigan Radio: http://michiganradio.org/post/legal-expert-examines-msu-s-potential-civil-and-criminal-liabilities-nassar-scandal

Statista (September 29, 2021). *Reported forcible rape rate in the United States from 1990 to 2020.* Retrieved from Statista: https://www.statista.com/statistics/191226/reported-forcible-rape-rate-in-the-us-since-1990/#statisticContainer

Stead Sellers, F., & Lamothe, D. (May 2, 2019). *Sexual assaults in the military spiked last year, Pentagon says, amid renewed debate over how to handle cases.* Retrieved January 3, 2020, from The Washington Post: National Security: https://www.washingtonpost.com/world/national-security/sexual-assaults-in-the-military-spiked-nearly-38percent-last-year-pentagon-says/2019/05/02/831826d8-5a11-11e9-842d-7d3ed7eb3957_story.html

Stedman, A. (November 23, 2014). *Ex-NBC Employee Claims He Helped Bill Cosby Pay Off Women.* Retrieved January 23, 2018, from Variety: http://variety.com/2014/tv/news/bill-cosby-sexual-assault-ex-nbc-employee-paid-off-women-1201363090/

Steffensmeier, D., Ulmer, J., & Kramer, J. (1998). The interaction of race, gender, and age in criminal sentencing: the punishment cost of being young, black, and male. *Criminology, 36*(4), 763–98.

Stewart, E. (March 7, 2019). *Sen. Martha McSally coming forward about her rape could be a watershed moment for Republican women.* Retrieved January 3, 2020, from Vox: https://www.vox.com/policy-and-politics/2019/3/7/18254575/martha-mcsally-raped-arizona-senator-republican

Stone, B. (March 27, 2017). *Alarming UT-Austin report: 15% of female undergrads say they've been raped.* Retrieved January 2, 2020, from USA Today: https://www.usatoday.com/story/college/2017/03/27/alarming-ut-austin-report-15-of-female-undergrads-say-theyve-been-raped/37429977/

Swartout, K., Koss, M., White, J., Thompson, M., Abbey, A., & Bellis, A. (December 12, 2015). Trajectory Analysis of the Campus Serial Rapist Assumption. *JAMA Pediatrics, 169*(12), 1148–54.

Swim, J., & Cohen, L. L. (1997). Overt, Covert & Subtle Sexism. *Psychology of Women Quarterly, 21*, 103–18.

Taschler, M., & West, K. (April, 2017). Contact with Counter-Stereotypical Women Predicts Less Sexism, Less Rape Myth Acceptance, Less Intention to Rape (in Men) and Less Projected Enjoyment of Rape (in Women). *Sex Roles*, 76, 473–84.

The Association of American Universities. (October 15, 2019). *AAU Releases 2019 Survey on Sexual Assault and Misconduct* . Retrieved April 11, 2021, from The Association of American Universities: https://www.aau.edu/newsroom/press-releases /aau-releases-2019-survey-sexual-assault-and-misconduct

Thompson, K. L., Hannan, S., & Miron, L. R. (October, 2014,). Fight, flight, and freeze: Threat sensitivity and emotion dysregulation in survivors of chronic childhood maltreatment. 69, 28–32.

Tillman, S., Bryant-Davis, T., Smith, K., & Marks, A. (April, 2010). Shattering Silence: Exploring Barriers to Disclosure for African American Sexual Assault Survivors. *Trauma, Violence & Abuse, 11*(2), 59–70.

Tinkler, J. E., Becker, S., & Clayton, K. A. (November, 2018). "Kind of Natural, Kind of Wrong": Young People's Beliefs about the Morality, Legality, and Normalcy of Sexual Aggression in Public Drinking Settings. *Law & Social Inquiry*, 43(1).

Tracy, N. (May 26, 2016). *Types of Rape: The Different Forms of Rape.* (H. Croft, Ed.) Retrieved November 5, 2017, from Healthy Place for Your Mental Health: https:// www.healthyplace.com/abuse/rape/types-of-rape-the-different-forms-of-rape/

Tsoulis-Reay, A. (December 1, 2015). *What It's Like to Be Chemically Castrated.* Retrieved January 6, 2020, from The Cut: https://www.thecut.com/2015/12/what -its-like-to-be-chemically-castrated.html

U.S. Department of Justice. (April 1, 2014). *Intersection of Title IX and the Clery Act.* Retrieved April 11, 2021, from U.S. Department of Justice: https://www.justice .gov/archives/ovw/page/file/910306/download

Ueda, M. (November, 2017). Developmental risk factors of juvenile sex offenders by victim age: an implication for specialized treatment programs. *Aggression and Violent Behavior, 37*, 122–128.

Ullman, S. (February, 2016). Sexual revictimization, PTSD, and problem drinking in sexual assault survivors. *Addictive Behaviors, 53*, 7–10.

Ullman, S., & Relyea, M. (August 23, 2016). Predicting Sexual Assault Revictimization in a Longitudinal Sample of Women Survivors: Variation by Type of Assault. *Violence Against Women, 23*(12), 1462–1483.

Union, G. (September 6, 2016). *Birth of a Nation' actress Gabrielle Union: I cannot take Nate Parker rape allegations lightly.* Retrieved November 18, 2017, from LA Times: http://beta.latimes.com/opinion/op-ed/la-oe-union-nate-parker-birth -nation-rape-allegation-20160902-snap-story.html

United States Department of Justice. (January 6, 2012). *An Updated Definition of Rape.* Retrieved August 30, 2020, from United States Department of Justice: https://www.justice.gov/archives/opa/blog/updated-definition-rape

Vagianos, A. (June 28, 2017). *Almost 850 Untested Rape Kits Found Growing Mold In Austin Police Storage: They were discovered amidst a statewide effort to address the backlog of rape kits.* Retrieved November 29, 2019, from Huffington Post: https://www.huffpost.com/entry/almost-850-untested-rape-kits-found-growing-mold-in-austin-police-storage_n_5953ce9ce4b0da2c73205a5f

Valentine, J. L., Sekula, L. K., Cook, L. J., Campbell, R., Colbert, A., & Weedn, V. W. (December 16, 2016). Justice denied: low submission rates of sexual assault kits and the predicting variables. *Journal of Interpersonal Violence, 34*(17), 3547–3573.

van Den Berg, C., Bijleveld, C., & Hendriks, J. (April 10, 2015). The juvenile sex offender. *Sexual Abuse: A Journal of Research and Treatment, 29*(1), 81–101.

van den Berg, J. W., Wineke Smid, J., Kossakowski, J., Daan van Beek, D., Borsboom, E. J., & Gijs, L. (2020). The application of network analysis to dynamic risk factors in adult male sex offenders. *Clinical Psychological Science,* 539–554.

Van Zandt, V. (January 28, 2021). *More Than 20 Teachers, Administrators Snared By Sexual Assault Claims In Just One School District.* Retrieved April 7, 2021, from Zenger: https://www.zenger.news/2021/01/28/more-than-20-teachers-administrators-snared-by-sexual-assault-claims-in-just-one-school-district/

Vandiver, D., & Teske, R. (2006). Juvenile female and male sex offenders. *International Journal of Offender Therapy and Comparative Criminology, 50*(2), 148–165.

Villalta, L., Khadr, S., Chua, K.-C., Kramer, T., Clarke, V., Viner, R. M., & Smith, P. (December 31, 2020). Complex post-traumatic stress symptoms in female adolescents: the role of emotion dysregulation in impairment and trauma exposure after an acute sexual assault. *European Journal of Psychotraumatology, 11*(1).

Volokh, E. (May 1, 2015). *The Volokh Conspiracy: Statutory rape laws and ages of consent in the U.S.* Retrieved November 10, 2017, from The Washington Post: https://www.washingtonpost.com/news/volokh-conspiracy/wp/2015/05/01/statutory-rape-laws-in-the-u-s/?utm_term=.4ba45a41d71e

Walsh, K., Messman-Moore, T., Zerubavel, N., Chandley, R., DeNardi, K., & Walker, D. (May, 2013). Perceived sexual control, sex-related alcohol expectancies and behavior predict substance-related sexual revictimization. *Child Abuse & Neglect, 37*(5), 353–359.

Waxman, O. (August 17, 2020). *It's a struggle they will wage alone. How Black women won the right to vote.* Retrieved from Time: https://time.com/5876456/black-women-right-to-vote/

Weiss, K. G. (April 1, 2013). "You just don't report that kind of stuff": Investigating teens' ambivalence toward peer-perpetrated, unwanted sexual incidents. *Violence and Victims, 28*(2), 288–302(15).

World Health Organization (2003). Guidelines for Medico-Legal Care for Victims of Sexual Violence.

Yan, H., & Burnside, T. (December 11, 2018). *Ex-Baylor frat president indicted on 4 counts of sex assault won't go to prison.* Retrieved December 20, 2019, from CNN: https://www.cnn.com/2018/12/11/us/baylor-ex-frat-president-rape-allegation/index.html

Yarbough, B. (January 14, 2021). *Why attorneys for California schools blame victims for their own sexual abuse, bullying* . Retrieved April 15, 2021, from Southern California News Group: https://www.mercurynews.com/2021/01/14/why-attorneys-for-southern-california-schools-blame-victims-for-their-own-sexual-abuse-bullying/.

Young, S. (December 22, 1997). The use of normalization as a strategy in the sexual exploitation of children by adult offenders. *The Canadian Journal of Human Sexuality*, 6(4), 285.

Zeitchik, S. (March 31, 2015). *Sexual assault complaint filed against film exec Harvey Weinstein*. Retrieved January 15, 2018, from Los Angeles Times: http://www.latimes.com/entertainment/movies/moviesnow/la-et-mn-harvey-weinstein-sexual-assault-allegation-20150330-story.html.

Zhu, N., & Chang, L. (2019). Evolved but not fixed: A life history account of gender roles and gender inequality. *Frontiers in Psychology*.

Zimmerman, A. (July 8, 2018). *How the Church of Scientology Went After Danny Masterson's Rape Accusers*. Retrieved July 10, 2018, from The Daily Beast: https://www.thedailybeast.com/how-the-church-of-scientology-went-after-danny-mastersons-rape-accusers.

Ziv, S. (November 23, 2017). *Danny Masterson Couldn't Have Raped Woman He Was Dating, Says Publicist*. Retrieved July 10, 2018, from Newsweek: http://www.newsweek.com/danny-mastersons-publicist-suggests-70s-show-actor-couldnt-have-raped-woman-he-721151.

Index

~

About the Author

Dr. Lisa R. Smith is a professor, author, and advocate who has taught psychology, sociology, criminal justice, and human service courses for twenty years. As a certified hypnotherapist, she helps at-risk youth and their families overcome trauma from PTSD, abuse (physical, sexual and emotional), and other mental health issues. As an author, she writes children's and academic books in which she uses her expertise and passion to spread the message of the importance of mental health to children, teens, and college students in the global market. A crusader against sexual assault and rape, she runs Right2Consent.com, a sex crime data collection website that encourages survivors of sexual victimization to report the crime to law enforcement.

www.ingramcontent.com/pod-product-compliance
Lightning Source LLC
Chambersburg PA
CBHW022321280326
41932CB00010B/1180